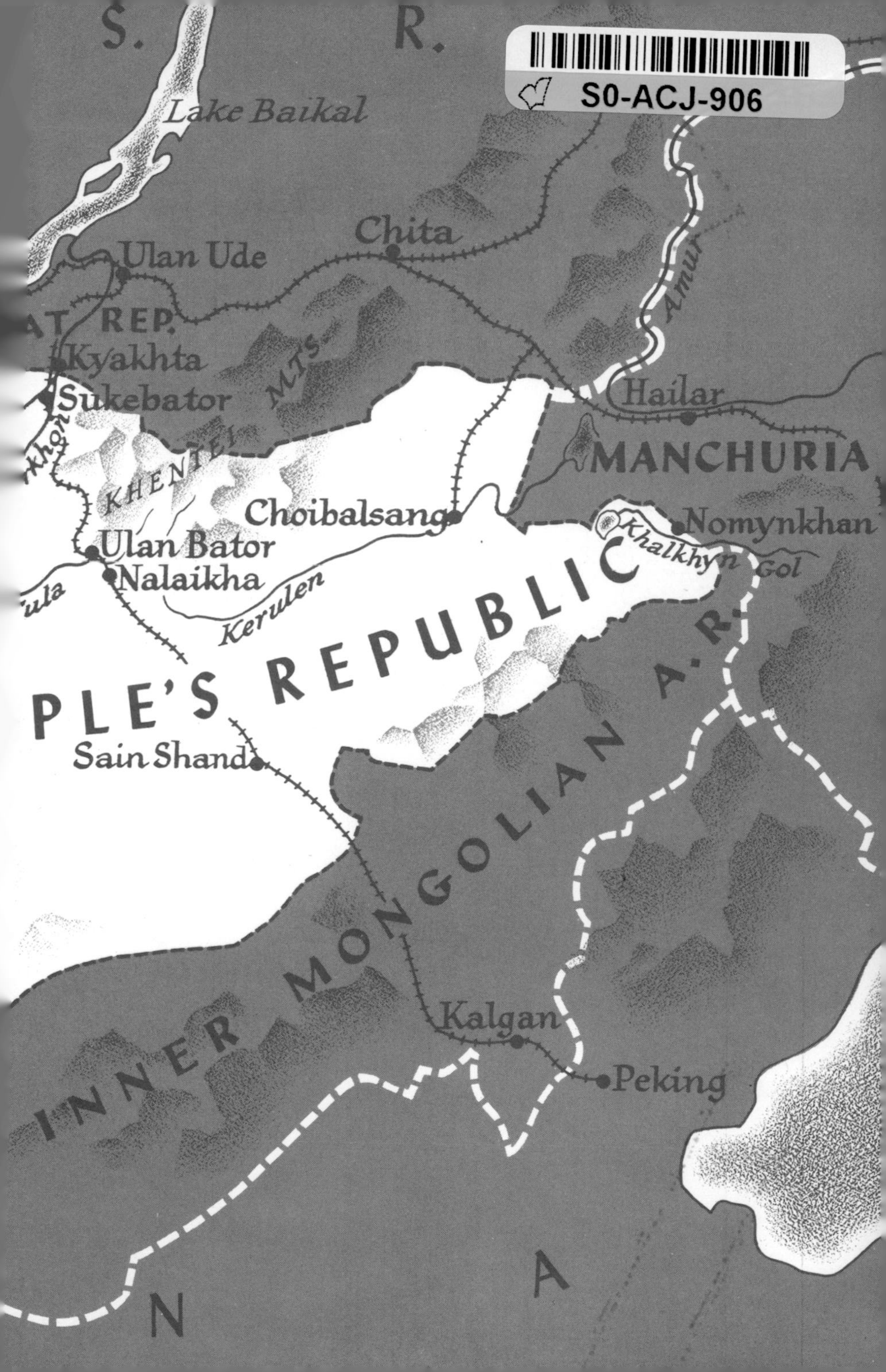
S. R.
Lake Baikal
Chita
Ulan Ude
AT REP.
Kyakhta
Sukebator
KHENTEI MTS.
Amur
Hailar
MANCHURIA
Choibalsang
Nomynkhan
Khalkhyn Gol
Ulan Bator
Nalaikha
Kerulen
Tula
PLE'S REPUBLIC
Sain Shand
INNER MONGOLIAN A.R.
Kalgan
Peking
A
N

Nomads and Commissars: Mongolia Revisited

Nomads and Commissars

MONGOLIA REVISITED

By OWEN LATTIMORE

New York · Oxford University Press

1962

Copyright © 1962 by Owen Lattimore

Library of Congress Catalogue Card Number: 62-16575

PRINTED IN THE UNITED STATES OF AMERICA

FOR ELEANOR

From Turkistan reunion in 1927
To Mongolia revisited in 1961

Contents

INTRODUCTION   xi

I   *The Then and the Now*   1

II   *"Mongolia's Lovely Land"*   16

III   *Nomads and Their History*   31

IV   *Autonomous Mongolia: The Years of Frustration*   50

V   *A Revolution of Shepherds*   75

VI   *The Real Revolution Begins*   92

VII   *The Worst Years*   122

VIII   *The Choibalsang Years*   148

IX   *Development, Transformation, Acceleration*   170

X   *Horseback Is All Right*   202

APPENDIX: *A Note on Sources and Supplementary Reading*   223

INDEX   231

Illustrations

THE ILLUSTRATIONS FOLLOW PAGE 134

Modern Ulan Bator—residential apartments

Old Ulan Bator—tents and stockades

Mongolia past and future: Hun's grave and Russian-made cars

Negdel in yak country

Mongol and horse

Modern Mongol woman

Modern Mongol worker with bicycle

Gandun monastery, Ulan Bator

Czechoslovak machinery at the "Kombinat"

Colts waiting for their mothers to be milked

Modern department store, Ulan Bator

Mongol tents, motorcycles

Monastery of Erdeni Jo in ancient capital, Karakoram

Amphibious vehicles of the Mongolian army

Headquarters of a negdel with slogans

Introduction

THE ADMISSION of the Mongolian People's Republic to
the United Nations in 1961 aroused sudden interest in
a country which, though it had not itself sealed its frontiers or made itself a hermit land, had been neglected
by the outside world for forty years. Mongolia's membership in the United Nations has led to the asking of many
questions. What are the relations between Mongolia and
the Soviet Union and China, the only countries with
which it has common frontiers? Is Mongolia a kind of
disguised member-republic of the Soviet Union? Or, on
the other hand, are the Mongols a kind of Chinese?
Is their language a dialect of Chinese? What is the difference between Outer Mongolia and Inner Mongolia?
Did anything ever happen in Mongolia between the
death of Chingis Khan, more than 700 years ago, and
our own times?

In this book I have written a general description of
what Mongolia and the Mongol people are like today,
with frequent references to historical phases of change

and development. It seemed to me that I ought to try my hand at such a book for two reasons. First, for more than thirty years Mongol studies have been a major part of my activities as a teacher and writer. Second, an unplanned encounter with some Mongol scholars in 1960, to which I shall refer again below, led to an invitation from the Mongolian Academy of Sciences to visit Mongolia in 1961, which provided me with a great deal of fresh material.

I have not gone into any details about international relations or diplomatic policy, because these are matters which are subject to rapid change. My hope is rather that when such things are discussed, people can turn to this book to find out something about the character of the country being discussed.

First, some background about things that will be referred to again and again.

Living in part of the vast area of historical migrations between Asia and Europe, the Mongols are physically a mixture of many stocks. (It is therefore unfortunate that "Mongol" and "Mongoloid" have come to be used as racial terms.) The Mongols are a different people from the Chinese, and their language is as unrelated to Chinese as English is to Finnish. The Mongol language is related to the Tungus family, of which Manchu is a member; it is more distantly related to Korean, and the nature of its relationship to the Turkish family of languages is a matter of controversy among scholars.

Formerly a part of the Manchu Empire, like China itself, Mongolia became autonomous in 1911, when both Mongols and Chinese revolted against Manchu rule. "Autonomy" was a status regulated by negotiations among three countries—Tsarist Russia, the Republic of

China, and Mongolia itself. China continued to claim sovereignty over Mongolia, however, until 1946, when Chiang Kai-shek agreed to a plebiscite in Mongolia, which was overwhelmingly in favor of complete independence and sovereignty. Chiang Kai-shek accepted this verdict, and China under Chiang voted in favor of Mongolia's first application for United Nations membership, later in 1946. This approval was withdrawn the very next year, however, because of a frontier dispute, and up to 1961 Chiang did his best to prevent Mongolia's admission to the United Nations. This objection was not based on a claim to sovereignty. It is not true, as many newspaper stories might lead the unwary reader to believe, that Chiang maintains that Mongolia is a province or possession of the island of Taiwan.

"Outer" and "Inner" Mongolia are old administrative terms. The Manchus conquered Inner Mongolia first, beginning with campaigns in the late 1500's, and Outer Mongolia much later; the consequence was that the administrative structure of Inner Mongolia was linked more closely than that of Outer Mongolia to the system that the Manchus set up in China. The old Outer Mongolia is the Mongolian People's Republic of today. The old Inner Mongolia has partly been absorbed by several Chinese provinces, and part of it has the status of an Inner Mongolian Autonomous Area, under Chinese sovereignty. This book deals with the Mongolian People's Republic, where my wife and I spent nearly two months in 1961, and has only incidental references to Inner Mongolia, which our government forbids Americans to visit, because it is a part of China.

After being autonomous from 1911 to 1921, Mongolia became *de facto* completely independent of China in

1921. This transition, which for the Mongols of today was "the" revolution, while that of 1911 was only a partial revolution, is discussed later in this book. In 1936 I first described Mongolia as a "satellite" of the Soviet Union, and since 1945 the term "satellite" has also been commonly applied to a number of other countries. Questions of "independence" and "satellitism" are also discussed later, but my main purpose in writing the book has not been to discuss political terminology but rather to describe conditions, characteristics, and, so to speak, the "behavior" of Mongolia as we saw them in 1961 and in the light of a long and fascinating history different from that of any other country.

What little I have to say about diplomatic questions might as well be said here. It has been suggested that it might be worth while for the United States to open diplomatic relations with Mongolia for the sake of obtaining a "listening post" or even a point of vantage from which to stir up trouble between the Soviet Union and China. This kind of argument is one of the sorry results of the Cold War. It is meant for domestic consumption and reflects the fear of being accused of "appeasement" in any attempt to ease relations with Communist-ruled countries. It substitutes false issues for real ones and only confuses public opinion.

There is no embassy, of any country, in any other country, that is not a listening post; and any embassy, of any country, can be used for stirring up trouble. That is a question of intention. In my opinion, the purpose of recognition should be to facilitate relations between the two countries concerned. In the case of the United States and Mongolia, both countries would benefit. It is as important for us that the Mongols should have a chance to know what we are like as it is for us to learn something about Mongolia. It is necessary for us to understand the relations of Mongolia with the Soviet Union and China if we want to know what kind of world we are living in. Mongolia is the only Communist-ruled country which is completely surrounded by other countries of the Communist bloc—Russia and China. In this respect it is different from Yugoslavia and Albania, from Hungary and Czechoslovakia, and also from Romania, which has one frontier with Yugoslavia. All four of these countries have at least one frontier with some country that is not in the Soviet bloc; but they are not all alike. Yugoslav policy is independent of Soviet policy, though often similar; Albanian policy is hostile to Soviet policy; Hungary and Czechoslovakia have somewhat different policies, but both are in line with Soviet policy. These differences are a reminder that Mongol policy needs to be studied in the light of Mongolian conditions. Mongolia should not be simply lumped together with all other Communist-ruled countries.

There is another aspect of Mongolia which should be of world-wide interest, and from which there is much that we could learn. The prosperous Mongolia of today is an example of development economics promoted through aid programs, by which a country formerly without machines or domestic capital is being rapidly modernized. While the aid is foreign, the development is highly national in the sense that the country can now rapidly take over new enterprises and staff them with its own personnel. The economy is in a boom of increasing prosperity. The political consequences are that the government is popular, and the alliance with Russia, the country principally responsible for the development program, is regarded by the people as their own alliance, not just a deal between politicians.

Things were not always so smooth; but things being as they now are, and lessons having been learned from mistakes made in the past, Mongolia may be increasingly looked to as an example by countries in Asia, Africa, possibly even Latin America, which are plagued with problems that have been solved, or appear on the way to being solved in Mongolia.

It is probable, and I should say often desirable, that problems in other countries should be solved by other methods; but the question of Mongolia comes down to this: if there is any country in the world in which any important problem has been solved, or even successfully tackled without yet being fully solved, I believe that representatives of our country should go there to study how it was done. If they decide that the solution was false or deceptive, they should so report.

My argument for the importance of Mongolia is a simple one. It is a country in which we might learn something. We are trying to teach, all over the world. A little willingness to learn would do us no harm with those we are trying to teach. The Mongols themselves are convinced that they are now qualified to teach peoples who are still as backward in one respect or another as they once were. (The Mongols were never backward in *all* respects.) But the Mongols are even more interested in continuing to learn. This applies expressly and explicitly to America. They are interested in our livestock handling, range management, and agriculture, as well as in our industry and technology. The gift of gifts, if you are visiting Mongolia, is an American book.

As I have already said, the opportunity to visit Mongolia in 1961 arose out of an unplanned encounter. In 1960 my wife and I attended the International Congress of Orientialists—one of those peripatetic congresses that is held each time in a different city. In 1960 it was held in Moscow. There was a Mongol delegation at the congress, and among them was Natsagdorj, a member of the Mongolian Academy of Sciences, whose biography of Sukebator, the founder of the Mongolian Revolution, I had translated a few years before.* These Mongols were very friendly, in an unforced, genuine way that made it easy for me to talk with them about historical problems which interested them and us. (They were also friendly with the other Americans who met them.) They suggested that, having got as far as Moscow, we ought to go farther and visit them in Mongolia. Another American who was at the Congress of Orientalists, Professor George B. Cressey of Syracuse University, a geographer with a special interest in deserts, did go on to Mongolia that year, but we had to tell the Mongols that we couldn't make it because we had to go instead to a Congress of the Historical Sciences in Stockholm. We would like to go in 1961, however. How would we get a visa? "Just let us know when your travel plans are definite," they said, "and then stop on your way and get a visa from the Mongolian Embassy in either Prague or Moscow."

The Mongolian delegation invited us to a dinner at which, following the social custom in all Communist

* See Owen Lattimore, *Nationalism and Revolution in Mongolia*, Leiden and New York, 1955, which includes a translation, by Owen Lattimore and Urgungge Onon, of the biography of Sukebator by Natsagdorj. (The spelling of this name in the old script, in which this biography was first published, is Nachukdorji.)

countries, the hosts got up at intervals between courses
to make polite little speeches. From this it became clear
that several of them knew English and had read some
of my publications, not just casually but with a scholar's
attention. One thing interested me particularly. People
like the Mongols, who frequently get called "primitive,"
"uncivilized," and so on, are often more irritated by
what is said about them in travel books than by political
opinions with which they do not agree; irritated in a
more personal way, that is. Now more than twenty years
ago the late Theodore Roosevelt, Jr., then of Double-
day, urged me to look into my old travel diaries and see
if I could write him a book about my experience of
Mongol life. I did, and in a mood of homesickness for
old scenes and old friends I put everything into the
book. The dirt and the lice were there, as well as a lot
of other things, but I was not looking down my nose or
feeling superior; I was trying to recall the feeling of
participation in a kind of life. So I was understandably
pleased when two of our Mongol friends referred especially to this book as a trustworthy account of what
Inner Mongolia was like in the 1930's. One of them
added, "your Mongols are real Mongols." *

When it was my turn to reply I mentioned, among
other things, the fact that they could hardly draw much
Marxist comfort from my writings. Then one of the
Mongols got up again, and said that all that was beside
the point. (This was a polite rebuke, as I realized after
thinking it over; after all, Marxists don't need to be
supplied with comfort by us non-Marxists; they have
their own built-in supply.) "What we like about your

* See Owen Lattimore, *Mongol Journeys*, New York and London, 1941.

work," our friend said, "is that you have a lot of ideas
that are strange to us. Sometimes you emphasize things
that we have taken so much for granted that we have
not particularly emphasized them. This we find stimulating, and it is a good thing. Besides, unless we compare
different judgments in selecting the facts, and different
opinions based on the facts, how are we to arrive at the
historical truth?"

With an open-minded reception like this promised in
advance, it was obvious that we must get to Mongolia if
we possibly could. As the expenses of such a long journey
would be beyond our means, I applied to the Wenner-
Gren Foundation for Anthropological Research and to
the American Philosophical Society (of which I am a
member) for support. In my application, I pointed out
that with the knowledge available it was impossible to
plan a definite piece of research. I should have to have
in mind a kind of general reconnaissance in the humani-
ties and the social sciences, to find out what the Mongol
scholars are doing in archaeology, in social and economic
history (in which the need for new work is more press-
ing than it is in political history), in cultural history,
and in anything else that might turn out to be interesting. In contemporary questions, my interest would be
largely in industrialization and development economics.

The enterprise would be a gamble. The auspices were
good, but in Communist-ruled countries the opportunities allowed to foreign scholars can be cut off abruptly.
It is therefore a special pleasure to record that both foun-
dations were willing to take a chance on our rather
nebulous enterprise. The Wenner-Gren Foundation
made a grant for the full amount asked, with no strings
attached except a request that my report should not

exceed one typewritten page in length, while the American Philosophical Society generously offered to hold their grant as a reserve fund in case we should run beyond our estimated expenses (which we did).

Our reception by the Mongolian Academy of Sciences was so open-handed that our success in our primary objectives was greater than could have been hoped. From my discussions with Mongol scholars and from printed material brought back I shall be able to make contributions to the Western stock of knowledge and ideas about such things as the origins of pastoral nomadism, a subject of importance in the Middle and Near East and North Africa, as well as Inner Asia. How far did the Mongolian form of it originate locally, and if so what preceded it? How far did it spread into Mongolia from elsewhere, and if so from where? These problems are associated with others like the rise of Chingis Khan and the origin of the Mongol conquests. Why did these conquests not take place a few hundred years earlier or later? Mongol scholars, as men themselves of nomad origin, have a special insight into these not yet fully written chapters of history. Because Chingis Khan shook the world—not only where his armies passed but all the way to the Vatican and the strongholds of the Teutonic Knights—these chapters interest everyone who seeks a world view of history.

At the same time I had from the beginning the idea, which grew stronger during our stay in Mongolia, of trying to write something that would place the Mongolia of today where it belongs: a deep background in which the story of the barbaric mounted shepherd bowman is interwoven with the highest cultural influences of China, India, Persia, and the Near East of Nestorian Christianity and Manichaeism. In modern times one must also take into account the Russian conquest and colonization of Siberia, the rise and fall of the Manchu Empire, and the rivalries of Western and Japanese imperialism. Contemporary problems include international competition in the development (which really means the modernization, the bringing into the twentieth century) of "underdeveloped" countries, distorted for us Americans by Madison Avenue phrases like "the competition for men's minds."

In what is going on throughout the world today there is, of course, a competition to win men's minds. Among the ways to reach men's minds there are logic (the reasoned argument for adventurous individual freedom against the dull conformity of the herd); sentiment (the family, the nation); and association (that of which we are proud because we received it from our ancestors and which we aspire to hand on to our descendants). But there is another way to men's minds, and that is through the material conditions under which they live. Are things bad, or good? Does it look as though they were going to get worse, or better than they were before? In either case, what can be done about it?

We Americans are prone to make a false distinction between "pure" and true spiritual values and "gross" material values. The truth is that both enter into human life, and are so tightly intertwined that they can never be neatly separated. Being well off has a lot to do with contented thinking. Being badly off may contribute either to discontented thinking or to resigned thinking. What makes the difference between action and passivity is often the feeling of a man, or a community, that things are likely to stay just about the same for an indefinitely long time, or will probably get so disastrously worse that there is not much use doing anything about it, or might get better if somebody does something about it. Here is where the material world in which we live joins with the theoretical world, with that which we abstract, by thought and emotion, from that which we know by experience.

In the world in which we live today, abstractions tend to become slogans—commercial or political. A typical slogan of our own world, appealing to the consumer, would be: Milk Builds Better Bodies—Buy More Milk. A typical slogan of the Communist world, specifically Mongolia, appealing to the producer, would be: Milk Is Wealth—Raise the Yield per Cow.

My problem, in writing about contemporary Mongolia, is to try to bring into focus a past which is rather hazy for us in the West—"primitive" shepherds, "romantic" warriors—and a turbulent present, in which the economics of development is used as a lever for the promotion of political aims. All through this 1961 visit I was uncomfortably aware of having certain advantages that might turn out to be serious disadvantages. Having first traveled in Mongolia (Inner Mongolia) more than thirty years ago; knowing the language; having read (and written) a great deal about the Mongols all through these years—the great danger would be the foregone conclusion: the danger of seeing evidence as the confirmation of opinions, when the true value of such a visit ought to be the opportunities it offers for discovering and correcting old mistakes, as well as adding new knowledge. The reader will have to judge for himself how well I have avoided pitfalls; but, as I said to our Mongol friends at our last meeting at the Academy of Sciences, if there are mistakes in this book, or things that they or anybody else considers wrong conclusions, they are honest mistakes and I apologize for them in advance; but they are not deliberate distortions.

O. L.

Ruxton, Maryland
June 1962

Nomads and Commissars: Mongolia Revisited

1

The Then and the Now

SOME OF THE Mongol students who had been with us on the train all the way from Moscow through Siberia brought along a new passenger "to see the Americans." He had got on at Sukebator, the first stop in the territory of the Mongolian People's Republic. He was one of those high-nosed Mongols who look like American Indians, and his skin was burned by wind and sun to a handsome coppery color. (I can still remember the incredulity of the late Ernest A. Hooton, of Harvard, in his time one of the great pundits of physical anthropology, when I told him that Chinese and Mongols, just like us, are paler when they live indoors and darker when they live an outdoor life.)

"So you learned your Mongol in Peking and Inner Mongolia?" said the newcomer. "Then you must know Chinese, too"—and he switched over, speaking a good, easy Chinese. "Russian, too? That's good. How about Korean?" I shook my head, and it was my turn to ask him how he had learned Korean. "From the Korean

ambassador and his chauffeur," he said, "they were pals
of mine when I was stationed in Ulan Bator."

Like most people in Communist countries, he didn't
mind personal questions, and told us that he had been
born in an ordinary shepherd family, had done his military service as a fighter-pilot, and had then gone to Russia
for training as an engineer. He had just finished building
the flour mill which dominates the skyline of Sukebator.
The machinery was Russian, but he had done the job of
building and installation with a labor battalion of 700
Chinese. "Good boys," he said. "I lived with them on
the job, and that's how I learned Chinese. We Mongols
always learn Chinese better than they learn our language.
We got the job done in a lot shorter time than the plan
called for, and now we're going on to build some
bridges."

In this brief encounter I was up against a number of
impossibilities—things unthinkable from the point of
view of a man who began to live and travel among the
Mongols more than thirty years ago. The first "impos-
sibility" was the idea of a railroad run by Mongols. It
was also unthinkable that a Mongol should be an aviator
or an engineer. Nor, in the old days, had anyone heard
of a Mongol bossing a lot of foreigners working for him
as laborers. And a man born in a shepherd family might
be pals with an ambassador's chauffeur, but not with the
ambassador.

So it was clear that my wife and I were entering a
Mongolia that was going to be quite new to us (though
we also found that a great deal of the old Mongolia
survives). In some ways, however, it was going to be
difficult to make comparisons. There are two Mongolias.
The Mongolian People's Republic is the Outer Mon-

golia of the nineteenth-century travelers. Even then, under the Manchu Empire, which fell in 1911, it had an administrative structure quite separate from, and different from, the provinces of China. South and southeast of this Mongolia is Inner Mongolia. Toward the end of the period of Manchu rule, and throughout the history of the Chinese Republic until the Communists took over in 1949, Inner Mongolia was divided into a number of sectors, each attached (and subordinated) to an adjoining Chinese province. The Chinese Communists have now created an Inner Mongolia Autonomous Area; but much of the historical Inner Mongolia was already completely Chinese, having long since been colonized by Chinese farmers.

It was the old Inner Mongolia of the 1920's and 1930's that my wife and I had known. Like all other travelers, what we had reported was a society and economy in decay. Most Mongols were poor. The economy was controlled by Chinese traders, who bought cheap and sold dear. There was no Mongol middle class, and the "intelligentsia"—which hardly deserved the name—consisted mostly of people with enough Chinese education to serve as minor bureaucrats, helping the Chinese to rule and exploit their own people. It is true that most of the men thus ignobly employed were bitterly resentful of their fate, and the fate of their people, but they were pathetically impotent.

Above the poor and the intelligentsia there was an aristocracy of hereditary nobles which had lost, to the Chinese, most of its functions as a ruling class, but retained many privileges of a feudal kind. It had therefore become merely parasitic; each noble family had families of herdsmen allocated to it who not only tended its cattle without pay but also provided it with many other kinds of unpaid services.

Finally, there was the Lama-Buddhist Church. This religion had become dominant in Mongolia only rather recently, as history in Asia goes, at the end of the sixteenth century, and from the seventeenth century on had been favored by the Manchu Emperors as a means of preventing Mongol unity and smothering Mongol nationalism. The Dalai Lama of Tibet can be described as the "Pope" of this religion, and the numerous "Living Buddhas" of Outer and Inner Mongolia as its "cardinal archbishops," but only if one adds the important qualification that the church had no centralized authority. Lhasa drew an immense revenue from Mongolia, but this flow of treasure was made up of the free-will offerings of the pious Mongols.

Mongolia was dotted with monasteries, and each important monastery was headed by a "Living Buddha," who was supposed to be the reincarnation of an attribute of Buddha himself, or of some Buddhist saint. When he died, it was said that the "vehicle" had perished, but the content of the vehicle was imperishable—it would be found again in a new vehicle, namely the body of a newborn child. By this device the monastery as a corporation became very powerful, because during the childhood of its new Living Buddha it ruled itself through a sort of committee of the senior lamas. It was this committee that controlled the selection of a child-Buddha; the Dalai Lama in Lhasa had no authority either to appoint or depose such "reincarnations," but the Manchu Emperor did exercise the prerogative of "confirming" the more important reincarnations—an excellent device for promoting disunity and corruption.

Marxists, of course—Mongol as well as Russian and Chinese—describe this church and all its institutions in the blackest terms, giving it no credit for the fact that it did produce a few truly saintly personalities, mystics, and great scholars, as did the medieval church in Europe. Only recently, since the church has lost all power and need not be feared, have a few Mongol scholars urged and actively undertaken the study of religious history as an important part of their country's cultural heritage. They now have government support for this program. It is only fair to add, however, that condemnation is not a Marxist or revolutionary monopoly. With the exception of a few devotees of mystic religion, all Tsarist Russian, Western, and Chinese travelers of the nineteenth and twentieth centuries described Mongolian Lamaism as ignorant, decayed, stagnant, superstitious, and economically parasitical.

They had good reason to. In both Inner and Outer Mongolia the church controlled about half of the national wealth—thus making impossible any realistic budget of the kind that a state has to have in the twentieth century. A monastery owned territory, and the herdsmen living in that territory were the subjects of the monastery and paid their taxes to it. About 40 per cent of the male population were priests. A man became a lama, or priest, because of the piety of his parents, not because of what we call "vocation." He was usually "presented" to a monastery as a child, perhaps eight years old, or even less. There he was assigned as a "disciple" to an older monk, who was supposed to teach him religion. Lamas could own property—money or cattle given to them by the pious. Inevitably this privilege, combined with the institution of discipleship, meant that a few lamas became rich and powerful and used as their own servants those who did not have either the knack of getting rich or the true vocation which leads a man to study the doctrines and texts of his religion.

Another important point was that the language of the religion was Tibetan, which is very different from Mongol. The possession of a special, holy language became one of the most important vested interests of the church, and made the lamas not only despise the secular history of their own people, written in the Mongol language, but obstinately oppose the teaching of the Mongol written language, except for the bare minimum needed by a few bureaucrats and tax-collectors. When 80 or 90 per cent of the people are illiterate, writing becomes Authority—and the church was jealous of any form of authority that might challenge its own hold over the minds of the people.

It is obvious that the Mongols of the twentieth century had either to modernize their society and state or perish as a people. If they stayed as they were, Inner Mongolia in the south would be taken over by Chinese colonists and Outer Mongolia in the north by Russian settlers. It is also obvious that even if Marx and Lenin had never lived, modernization of any kind would have been impossible without a showdown fight between church and state and also, and at the same time, an economic and social revolution. In other words Henry VIII of England, if he had been granted a Buddhist reincarnation in twentieth-century Mongolia, would immediately have recognized the situation. Was the state going to be the boss, or the church?

For several hundred years, while the rest of the world changed, the Mongols had been stagnant, and for at least a hundred years Mongolia had suffered something worse than stagnation; its economy and society had decayed and fallen below their own previous level, principally because of the draining off of wealth by Chinese traders and the church. If the Mongols did not get on terms with the changed, twentieth-century world around them, their fate would be that of the American Indian. If they were to force their way into the twentieth century it meant telescoping into a few years, which were bound to be years of terrible suffering, everything that Europe went through in the Reformation and the wars of religion, and at the same time the kind of disruption that Europe went through in the Industrial Revolution.

But while these facts are obvious, they are not facts of a kind that can be documented in an easy, simple statistical way. This rapid summary is enough to show the kind of problem that my wife and I faced. We had known the Inner Mongolia of the 1920's and 1930's. But now we weren't in Inner Mongolia, which we could compare with its own past; we were in Outer Mongolia, the Mongolian People's Republic. It is true that I had been in Ulan Bator, the capital, for about three days in 1944 when I accompanied Vice President Henry A. Wallace on a wartime mission to Siberia, Soviet Central Asia, and China *—but three days doesn't add up to a claim to first-hand knowledge. Now we were going to have to try to square what we saw during our visit with an account of how things got that way, derived not from personal experience but from what people told us, and from documents. We were not going to be able to introduce questions by saying "When we were here before. . ."

From the beginning of this century Mongolia has

* See Henry A. Wallace, *Soviet Asia Mission,* New York, 1946.

become more and more closely associated with Russia—
a development which began when Russia was under
Tsarist rule, accelerated when a Soviet state was established in Russia and a state closely akin to it in Mongolia, and accelerated again at the end of the Second
World War, when the menace of Japanese imperialism
was lifted. This development is a reversal of Mongolia's
previous history, which had always been oriented toward
China. For the Mongols, whether they were attacking it
or defending themselves against it, whether it was ruled
by a dynasty of Chinese origin or a dynasty of barbarian
conquerors, China was always the land of a great nation
—*the* great nation. Siberia, on the other hand, was only
a land of tribes, weaker and more dispersed than the
tribes of the Mongols themselves, because people who
lived in the main by hunting in the Siberian forests, even
if they also kept a few cattle and did a little desultory
farming, had to scatter out even more widely and thinly
than the herdsmen of Mongolia.

No tribe could assemble in the forests of Siberia in
numbers large enough to make itself a nation. As for
the Mongols themselves, if they migrated into Siberia
as did the ancestors of the Buryats of the Lake Baikal
region, they tended thereby to change in a way which
made them, in the eyes of the Mongols of Mongolia,
"less Mongol." When Buryats use the term "Mongol,"
it means for them "the larger family of which we are
an offshoot"; but the Mongols of Mongolia, if they grant
the name "Mongol" to the Buryats at all, do so a little
doubtfully, and this has been true for some centuries.
For them, the name "Buryat" means very definitely
"people who are different from us Mongols." At the
present time the Russians have stopped using the term

"Buryat-Mongol Republic." It is now "the Buryat Republic"; but this is only an institutional confirmation of a change that has been a long time in the making.

When the thrust of Chingis Khan's conquests carried the Mongols all the way to Russia, they marched through the lands of ancient oasis civilization in the Middle East, and across the steppes of Turkistan and southern Siberia —not by the northern line through the great forests. The Russians whom the Mongols dimly remembered from this chapter of their history were quite different from the Cossack bands which began to appear among the Buryats and on the northern frontier of Mongolia in the late 1500's. These Cossacks must, at first, have seemed to the Mongols to be just another tribe—formidable because of their firearms, but not menacing the Mongols with conquest.

At this very time, morever, there was a menace which the Mongols did fear—the rising power of the Manchus, who were already gathering for the conquest of China and already extending their authority over the Mongols of Inner Mongolia, partly by conquest and partly by diplomacy and alliances. It was always the policy of the Manchus to assert in China that they were worthy heirs of China's civilized tradition, but to represent themselves in Mongolia as "more like" the Mongols than the Chinese. The Mongols saw it differently. For them, the power of the Manchus was the power of China. Under the Manchus, China was becoming once more "the great nation," and the Mongols rightly feared that the Manchu conquest of China would be followed by a Chinese conquest of Mongolia. The Manchus established themselves in Peking in 1644, but it took more than another century and several great campaigns, complicated and

embittered by wars between the Oirats or Ölöts of
western Mongolia and the Khalkhas who form the main
body of the Mongol people, before the Manchus could
establish complete authority over the whole of Mongolia—a Mongolia which was by then devastated and
impoverished.

It is this delay which accounts for the difference be
tween "Inner" and "Outer" Mongolia. Geographically,
Inner Mongolia is the area which the Manchus first
attached to their conquest in China; in fact, many Inner
Mongolian tribes were used as auxiliaries in that conquest; while the delay in time in extending the conquest
to Outer Mongolia resulted in important institutional
differences. Instead of the administrative system of Inner
Mongolia being simply enlarged to take in Outer Mongolia, a new set of institutions was drawn up. Institutional differences, in turn, contributed to an increasing
general differentiation, comparable but not identical
with the increasing difference between Mongols and
Buryats. As in the case of the Buryats, many Mongols of
Inner Mongolia like to stress the theme of common
Mongolness, while the Mongols of Outer Mongolia tend
more and more to think of them as a different people.

In all this time, there was no threat of a Russian invasion of Mongolia to rival or anticipate the Manchus. The
trend was, in fact, in the other direction. Many Mongols
fled into Siberia and merged with the Buryats, and more
would have gone if the Russians had let them enter.
From time to time, also, one or another Mongol chieftain
would raise the question of offering allegiance to the
Russian Tsar. The Russians of that time regarded the
power of the Manchu Empire with great respect—a respect which began to diminish only after the defeat of

China by the British in the Opium War of 1840-42. And when they did begin to expand at the expense of China it was not by going into Mongolia but by pushing through what was then a no-man's-land (though vaguely claimed by the Manchus as part of their ancestral tribal domain) and establishing their frontiers along the Amur and Ussuri rivers. In the late seventeenth and early eighteenth centuries the Russians from time to time placated the Manchus by preventing Mongol refugees from entering Siberia, and even returned to Manchu rule Mongols who had settled among the Buryats.

Out of this balance of forces there developed a Mongol national outlook: China, either under Manchu rule or under Chinese rule, was to be feared. Russia was not to be feared. Quite the contrary, in fact; the Russians, if properly approached, might be helpful. It is this national outlook that explains why, when the Manchu Empire fell in 1911, the theocratic and feudal government which the Mongols then organized was not only willing but eager to put itself under the patronage of Tsarist Russia; and why, when that government had been defeated and discredited by a Chinese war lord who forced it to declare Mongolia once more a part of the Chinese Republic, the new, revolutionary leadership which then arose was equally eager to put itself under the tutelage of the Russian revolutionaries.

But why did the Russians, even when China was weakest, as in 1911-12, never try to annex Mongolia? The Russians of today as Marxists, categorically condemn imperialism: it is always greedy, always expansive. This prevents them from recognizing that imperialisms from time to time go into phases of self-limitation, in which they seek to define their frontiers instead of expanding

them. This occurs when imperialism runs into diminish-
ing returns, and the costs of expansion in a particular
direction begin to become bigger than the profits. It
explains why the Chinese built the Great Wall and why
the Roman Empire fortified its Rhine-Danube frontier
and built walls to separate England and Scotland.

Up to the Russo-Japanese War of 1904-05 Britain and
Russia had been rivals. Although this rivalry had been
mitigated by the Pamir Agreement of 1895, defining
boundaries in Central Asia, the British still had an exaggerated fear of Russian intrigue in Tibet. It was to forestall the Russians, as he thought, that Lord Curzon, then
Viceroy of India, sent the Younghusband Expedition to
Lhasa in 1903-04. But almost immediately after this
Russia was defeated by Japan, and weakened by this
defeat and by its own 1905 Revolution it was no longer
feared by Britain. There then began the regrouping of
forces which was to put Britain and Russia on the same
side in the First World War: Britain, while remaining
an ally of Japan, came to an understanding with Russia
that included the British position in Tibet and the Russian position in Mongolia.

In stabilizing their relations with each other after
1905, Tsarist Russia and Japan signed several secret
treaties (which have since been published).* These
treaties allocated North Manchuria as a Russian sphere
of influence, and South Manchuria as a Japanese sphere
of influence, and took the meridian of Peking, which
very roughly corresponds with the eastern frontier of
Mongolia, as the dividing line between Russian interests
on the west and Japanese interests on the east. In the

* Ernest B. Price, *The Russo-Japanese Treaties of 1907-1916
Concerning Manchuria and Mongolia*, Baltimore, 1933.

situation thus constructed most people at that time expected Japan, by developing the resources of Manchuria,
to become a very powerful country. Russia, committed
to imperial rivalry with Japan by exploiting North Manchuria, had neither the money nor the manpower to
exploit Mongolia in the same way. Moreover, the economic structure of Manchuria was of a kind that gave
quick returns on capital investment, while that of Mongolia required heavy investment and a long wait before
seeing attractive profits. Nor was the settlement of Russian colonists in Mongolia a practical policy: the Russians
at that time were paying out a lot of money to subsidize
internal colonization in Siberia, and while some of them
may have thought of colonizing Mongolia in the future,
they could only have been thinking of a distant future.

The obvious policy for Tsarist Russia was therefore
to use Mongolia as a large, almost empty buffer zone,
isolating it from the western limits of Japanese expan-
sionism in South Manchuria and from the large population of China, which at this time was beginning the rapid
colonization of Inner Mongolia. This was a policy that
harmonized well with that of Britain in Tibet, for what
Britain wanted was also a buffer zone which would prevent the establishment of a Chinese population at the
Himalayan edge of India. If Britain had had to maintain
on this frontier armed forces as large as those along the
North-West Frontier with Afghanistan, the expense
would have been crippling.

Therefore, when the Manchu Empire fell in 1911
and both Mongolia and Tibet tried to break away from
China, Russia and Britain were well pleased. Russia did
not want full independence and sovereignty for Mongolia, however, nor did Britain want it for Tibet. What

each country wanted was a protected area inhabited by
people who were not Chinese, enjoying enough autonomy or self-government to keep out Chinese officials and
Chinese colonists. There would be no trouble in controlling these protectorates: they would be so weak that
they would never cease to fear Chinese attempts to re-
assert authority over them, and would therefore of their
own accord turn constantly to their protectors for advice.
The correctness of this reasoning was shown by the fact
that, when Russia refused to back Mongol demands for
full independence, one of the alternative proposals con-
templated by the Mongols was that Russia should annex
them, and then give them the same kind of autonomy
that Finland had under Tsarist rule!

The policies of a great power have a tendency to be
continuous, even after a revolution. The Soviets inherited
the Tsarist buffer-zone policy in Mongolia, and continued in large measure to practice it right up to the end
of the Second World War. To Chinese claims that the
autonomy of Mongolia was a work of Tsarist imperialism and that the Soviet Russians, as good revolutionaries,
ought to return it to Chinese rule, the Soviet reply was,
in essence: "We are not imperialists. We are not going
to annex Mongolia. We are prepared to recognize your
claim to full sovereignty over Mongolia; but it is not our
business to enforce it for you. In the meantime, here are
the Mongols, right on our frontier. They are our neighbors. We have to deal with them because they are there;
and they claim full sovereignty and independence, not
just autonomy. There is also the fact that you are torn
apart by war-lord politics. We recognize your national
government, but we—and you—have to face the fact that
it does not control the northern war lords whose prov-

inces control the various sectors of Inner Mongolia. You therefore do not even have access to Mongolia.

"Moreover, there is a common danger to you, to the Mongols, and to us. It comes from the ambitions of Japanese imperialism. It would be bad for you, and it would be very dangerous for us, if the Japanese were to conquer Mongolia. The Mongols say that if the Japanese attack, they will resist. That being so, we shall certainly help them, by equipping and training their army and by economic and other programs that will strengthen them as allies."

Soviet Russia continued this policy until, as one of the consequences of the Yalta Conference, Chiang Kai-shek (with American approval) agreed to a plebiscite to determine the question of sovereignty in Mongolia. The genuineness of this vote has sometimes been questioned, because of the mistaken notion that it meant "a vote for Russia"; but the only question the plebiscite was asked to decide was that of Mongolian independence *versus* Chinese rule—and of course the Mongols voted joyfully and overwhelmingly for independence. The decision of the plebiscite was accepted and ratified by the government of Chiang Kai-shek, a fact which became very important later, because it meant that among the nationalistic claims which the Chinese Communists took over when they defeated Chiang Kai-shek there was no longer a claim to Mongolia.

These changes open up other political questions, but they will be dealt with later. It is time now to turn to a consideration of what kind of country Mongolia is.

2

"Mongolia's Lovely Land"

High lovely ridges of the Khentei, Khangai, Soyon,
Thick-wooded mountains, the beauty of the north;
The wide great Menen, Sharga, Nomin gobi-spaces
And seas of sand-dunes fronting on the south:

This, this is the home where I was born—
Mongolia's lovely land.

—DASHDORJIIN NATSAGDORJ
(1906-37)

NOMADS BY RIGHT of uncounted centuries of inheritance,
the Mongols of today retain much of that inheritance,
in spite of the growth of agriculture and the rapid spread
of industry.

Living parts of their tradition—the "Three Manly
Sports" of the Mongols, which they practice and follow
passionately—are horse-racing, archery, and wrestling.
All three come down to them from their military and
tribal past. To them might well be added poetry, which
also represents an unbroken tradition: the *Secret History
of the Mongols*, the great thirteenth-century chronicle

which combines legends from much more ancient times with vivid details of the life of Chingis Khan, contains many passages of fine poetry, composed not with rhyme at the end of the line but with alliteration at the beginning, in a verse form that often recalls the Scandinavian sagas and could conceivably have been influenced by very ancient Indo-European contacts.

Summer, when there is least work to do and the pasture is at its best, is the horse-racing season. The most important part of the training is an alternation of exercise—to build up the horse's strength—with starvation—to bring down the size of its belly—because a horse that feeds only off the lush pasture and is given no grain easily puts on a belly that is too big for fast galloping. There are separate races for stallions, for amblers, and for age classes (two-year-olds, three-year-olds, and so on), but the great race is that for mature horses of six years and upward. Good horses have been known to go on winning races up to the age of about twenty.

The two things that set Mongol racing altogether apart are the length of the race and the age of the jockeys. Both are accounted for by history. The Mongols, once the world's greatest long-range raiders and cavalrymen, are not as much interested in sprinting as they are in stamina, and therefore the races are over distances of 19 miles (25 kilometers) or 38 miles (50 kilometers). As for the jockeys—they are children from six to nine years old—and girls may ride as well as boys. In the big races, children over nine are barred, though in Inner Mongolia I have seen races in which teen-agers were allowed. The reason for this is that the Mongols want the race to bring out the horse's willingness and heart, as well as his capacity. They therefore do not want a

jockey strong enough to force the horse, but only someone to guide him. It is exciting, in the last mile of a long
race, to see the differences among the horses, especially
those which seem to pull from somewhere a reserve of
strength and start a rush from behind to overhaul and
pass the leaders—but it is not always all in the horse; it is
uncanny what precocious horsemen some of the little
children are, knowing how to calm down the excitement
of the horse in the early stages of the race and rouse it
again as the finish comes in sight.

My wife and I went out one day to watch the finish of
one of the big races. Big blue pavilion-tents, decorated
with white scroll ornaments, had been pitched to shade
those who felt the heat too much. In the open sunlight,
the air was spicy with the aroma of the pasture—artemisia,
I think, was one of the principal perfumes. It, and several
species of wild garlic and wild onions, and a plant that
has a smell something like sage, give Mongolian mutton
a flavor that eaters of the prim American lamb chop cannot even imagine.

Here I met a man, old and sick, sitting with his face
turned gratefully to the sun, the breast of his blue gown
covered with medals. To my intense interest, he was
Sodnomdarjaa, one of the most famous Partisans of
1921 and the leader of a raid, several years later, into a
no-man's-land region on the borders of Inner and Outer
Mongolia to put an end to Dambijantsan, the "False
Lama" who for years had terrified western Mongolia.*
I wanted to ask him about this, but he was too tired and
weak. "I haven't much time left," he said patiently. A
couple of weeks later my wife and I were in a guest-tent

* See the chapter on "The House of the False Lama," in Owen
Lattimore, *The Desert Road to Turkestan*, Boston, 1928.

far out in the west when the news of his death came over the radio. When our Mongol hosts came in and I told them the news, every man was as subdued as if a close relative had died. "He was the most loved of the Partisans," they said.

The pasture looked south to a long ridge, wooded on its northern side, the old Holy Mountain of the Living Buddhas of Urga, now renamed the Choibalsang Mountain. To the west was rolling country, where we now saw a dust plume rising. The horses were coming, and we all moved toward the line along which they would pass. More than a hundred had started, but the long race had strung them out—three or four, well-spaced, in the lead, then clusters of eight, ten, twenty. The child jockeys were swinging their whips rhythmically, but by now without much strength, hitting the horse first on the left haunch, then on the right, and, in the same rhythm, ululating in a thin treble screech what must have been a child's version of an ancient war cry.

In the old days the winners were led at once before whatever dignitary was presiding over the races, but now this is done on the afternoon of the same day, or the morning of the next day, in the great modern stadium. The winning riders, usually four, canter the full circuit of the stadium, each accompanied by a herald in a rose silk gown. They pull up in front of the grandstand and each child is offered a large bowl of fermented mare's milk, from which he drinks, then pours some on the rump of his horse. As he does so, each herald in turn chants, in a poem which he has composed, the name of the horse, the region from which it comes, its previous victories, its special qualities of character and courage, the name of the owner, and the name of the child jockey.

Then, each in turn, the children are lifted off their horses by their heralds and ushered up into the grand-stand, "their little hearts bursting with pride," as an English author describes it,* to receive their prizes.

The poetry is not perfunctory. Once when I was listening, the heralds who presented the first horse and the second each received their due round of applause, but while the third herald was chanting I noticed the people near me getting tense. What had been a polite, attentive silence deepened into the rare stillness of an audience that is aware of something great, and as the poem ended the whole stadium exploded in applause. The horse had run only third, but the herald's poem had won a brilliant first.

Wrestling is I think the most national of all Mongol sports. It excites and combines the same kinds of passion that some people in the United States have for boxing and others for baseball or, elsewhere, for soccer football. There is practically no such man as a Mongol who has not wrestled in boyhood and early manhood. Every spectator understands the fine points. Every hold and every throw has its name. Every champion's career is remembered, and people talk about the details of matches years ago. The style is somewhat similar to English Cumberland-Westmorland wrestling. Each wrestler wears heavy boots, a very small, tight-fitting loin-cloth, and a pair of sleeves which meet across the back of his shoulders in some-thing resembling a tiny vestige of a jacket. (In Inner Mongolia the jacket is much larger, and covered with metal studs, against which a man will grind his oppo-nent's face if he gets the chance.)

* Ivor Montagu, *Land of Blue Sky*, London, 1956, p. 154.

As the contestants come out on the field they go into an ungainly leaping, sprawling dance, flapping their arms. This is said to be in imitation of an eagle, or a buzzard. Each wrestler has his attendant herald, who in important matches chants in poetry the heroic attributes of his champion. As each man goes to meet his opponent, his hat is taken off his head by his herald. All during the match, the herald stays close to his man. He can appeal to the umpires if he thinks there has been a foul. At the end of the match, the herald "caps" the winner by putting the hat back on his head.

A match is won when any part of the loser's body except the soles of his feet touches the ground. The opening hold is a head-to-shoulder hold in which each man grasps his opponent by the upper sleeve, or by the "jacket" across the back of his shoulders. As some men prefer to have their arms above the other man's arms, while some others prefer the under-grip, there is often a lot of sparring before both men take hold. The grip may later be shifted to take hold of the other man's loin-cloth, or to grab a leg. A kind of side-swiping kick is allowed, to knock the other man's leg or legs from under him, but a kick with the toe of the boot against the other man's shin is not allowed.

Strategically the best posture for a wrestler is to keep his center of gravity a little lower than his opponent's, so as to be steadier and in a position to heave upward or drag sideways at the right opportunity; but not so low as to enable the other man to pile on top and crush him to the ground. For these reasons much of the time is spent, if the match is a long one, with the two men locked head to shoulder, backs curved in an arch, legs well straddled, and feet far back and out of reach of the other man's feet. Some men maneuver for a long match, wearing the other man down slowly for half or three-quarters of an hour; others prefer quick shifts of weight and position to get the other man off balance and end perhaps by flinging him through the air, sideways or over the shoulder.

Archery has as ancient a history as wrestling; both are mentioned in the *Secret History of the Mongols,* and an inscription on stone, a little older than the *Secret History* and also of the thirteenth century, records an arrow shot of 335 "spans," which has been estimated as about 500 meters. The Mongols use a compound bow, built up of layers of horn, sinew, bark, and wood. When unstrung it is not straight, like an English longbow, but is curved as if it were a bow strung with an invisible string. To string it, the two ends are bent back in the opposite direction, so that the bow when strung is the reverse of the unstrung bow. The result is a bow short enough to be handled on horseback, but at least as powerful as the English longbow. The arrow carries three ribs of feathering, set a little bit asymetrically, which make the arrow turn with a screw-motion in flight, like a bullet from a rifle, and make it penetrate deeper when it hits the target. Archery is more archaic and ritualistic than the other sports. All archers take the same stance and posture. The bow is held parallel to the ground, with the arrow on the string, while being raised to shoulder height; only then is it turned vertically into the normal shooting position, one end up and the other down, while the string is being drawn back. The target provides an exercise in trajectory; instead of being round and set up on a frame or easel, like our targets, it is a low line of blocks of wood, painted red. The favorite distance seems to be about a hundred yards, so that the arrow has to rise well into the air, descend in a curve, and hit the low target without overshooting or undershooting. While the arrow is in the air the long lines of spectators raise a wailing, keening cry which ends on a note of triumph if the shot is good, or despair if it is bad. Women compete against women, not against men, but they use the same bows as the men and shoot at the same distance. The sport has an irresistible fascination. At the end of a round of shooting visitors pile out of the grandstand— Russians, Poles, Czechs, East Germans; everybody except the staid, formal, unsmiling Chinese—to try a shot. It isn't easy to be as graceful and skilled as the Mongols. Most of the visitors' arrows wobble off course, or fall short.

The "lovely land" of these heirs of the past is a country of a little over 600,000 square miles—almost three times the size of France, almost exactly the total combined area of France, Germany, Italy, and England; two and a quarter times the size of Texas. Here live a little less than one million people, whose herds of sheep, goats, horses, cows, yaks, and camels number about 23 million. Mongolia has only two frontiers—one with the Soviet Union, one with China. The whole length of the frontier with the Soviet Union has been completely resurveyed and fixed; that with China has still to be finally determined.

Although Mongolia is south of Siberia, it is still a northern land. Its northernmost point is not quite as far north as Moscow, or Edmonton, Alberta. Its southernmost point is not quite as far south as New York City.

In the east, it does not quite stretch as far as the longitude of Shanghai, and in the west it reaches roughly the longitude of Calcutta. It is just about twice as long from east to west (approximately 1600 miles) as it is deep from north to south (approximately 800 miles). It is also a high country, tilted from the mountains of the west to the plains of the east. The average elevation is 4800 feet above sea level, which may be compared with "mile-high" Denver, Colorado—5280 feet. The lowest point, in the northeastern plains not far from where the frontiers of Mongolia, Siberia, and Manchuria join, is 1682 feet; the highest, the peak of Kuiten ("Cold Mountain") in the Altai range in the far west, is 14,181 feet. (Mount Whitney, in California, is 14,502 feet; Mont Blanc is 15,782 feet.)

Mongolia's river system shows the country's triple relationship to Siberia and the Arctic Ocean, to China's Manchurian provinces and the Pacific, and to the "dead heart" of innermost Asia, from which no rivers reach any sea, but wither away in deserts and salt lakes. Twelve major rivers are listed as contributing their waters to the Arctic Ocean. Of these the longest is the Orkhon, with 700 miles, entirely in Mongol territory, but the most important is the Selenga, into which the Orkhon flows—because it carries a traffic of small river-steamers; it empties into Lake Baikal, in Siberia, which through the Angara, joining the Yenesei, drains to the Arctic Ocean.

Of the four rivers which flow to the Pacific through the Amur, the northern boundary between Manchuria and Siberia, the longest is the Kerulen (over 600 miles in Mongolia, over 100 miles in Siberia). Of the rivers whose waters never reach an ocean, the longest is the Dzabkhan—500 miles—in the west.

There are also important lakes in Mongolia, mostly of an Alpine character, in the northwest. The largest is Ubsu Nur, with an area of over 1200 square miles, and the next largest is Khubsugul (the "Kossogol" of most maps) with about 1000 square miles. These lakes, and many of the rivers, are rich in fish, which were not eaten by the Mongols in the past, because of an aversion amounting almost to a taboo. Mongols are now increasingly eating fish, but some of the old prejudices linger. Talking at breakfast over a large, very tasty fish from the Orkhon River with a Mongol who had traveled widely in China (learning the know-how of running a large health resort), I said, "Did you notice how, in China, with a fish like this, the real tid-bit is the eyes?" "Yes, I know," he replied, "but I couldn't quite bring myself to it. Somehow, it's not like a boiled sheep's eye, which is both tasty and good for what ails you."

Cut off from the sea by the full width of China's Manchurian provinces, Mongolia has a strongly continental climate, and because of its height the winter is all the colder. Ranges of both temperature and rainfall are extremely wide. Traveling by camel in rather low-lying country in Inner Mongolia, near the southwestern frontier of the Mongolian People's Republic, I have walked about in the open stripped to the waist in the middle hours of the day in December, but as the sun got low we all huddled in sheepskins, and at night (I had no thermometer) tea poured into a wooden bowl would freeze within a few feet of the fire in the middle of the tent.

The severity of the climate is shown by the fact that the average, all-year round temperature of Ulan Bator, the capital, is a little below freezing. Unfortunately, the available figures do not show how many months are frost-free; but in the years from 1941 to 1960 the highest temperatures of the year at Ulan Bator have frequently reached 90° Fahrenheit, while in winter they have plunged to 50° below zero. Yet the best wheat-growing districts are north, not south of Ulan Bator—because this is the zone in which a June-July-August rainy season, sometimes extending into September, combined with the maximum sunlight hours of long, northern summer days, makes for the rapid growth and maturing of grain in a short season. For those who think of Mongolia as mostly desert, it is worth noting that in this zone, if the rainy season is late and lasts too long, there is even the danger that the grain will rot in the fields before it ripens. To regulate this uncertainty, irrigated agriculture has from ancient times been intermittently practiced, in order to give the grain a good early start. In the sheltered Kobdo basin in the northwest even irrigated rice is grown; and this is not a new, revolutionary introduction but a traditional occupation of Turkish-speaking Uighur immigrants from Sinkiang (Chinese Turkistan). The alternation of periods of flourishing agriculture and abandoned agriculture is an important but hitherto neglected theme of Mongol history. Altitude is also a critical factor. At the present time, oats are being planted in western Mongolia at heights where the early frost makes ripening impossible; they are harvested unripe, as cattle-feed.

Mongolia's climate is powerfully affected in the north

by the Siberian weather system of rainfall and snow, and in the south by the fringes of China's monsoon system. The differences between the two are best illustrated by two Mongol terms, *khangai* and *gobi*. Foreigners call a highland massif in west-central Mongolia *the* Khangai, and the arid zone that runs along the south of Mongolia *the* Gobi, or "the Gobi Desert." For Mongols, however, the Khangai is merely a region in which there are lots of khangais, and the Gobi a region in which there are lots of gobis.

A khangai is a stretch of highland territory in which the mountains are of medium height and rounded, not craggy; there are wooded slopes of larch and pine, plenty of streams, and prairies and meadows in wide, shallow valleys which give rich pasture. The patches of forest are what make a khangai, and here there is an important distinction. In the administrative province that is now called North Khangai (Ar-Khangai), the forest is always on northerly slopes; in South Khangai (Öbör-Khangai, often written Uber-Khangai), on southerly slopes. This is because in one case the moisture comes from Siberia, and is precipitated when it strikes a mass of land that is high enough, in the other case it is borne over inland China by winds that have strayed from the coastal monsoons, crosses the low-lying gobi zone, and is precipitated when it hits southward-facing slopes. Height is extremely critical for the flourishing of khangai forest. At the right height, the trees grow vigorously; in a zone extending only a couple of hundred feet lower they dwindle and become stunted; then they stop completely, along a cleanly marked line. I had formerly thought that the gobi zone was the climatic frontier in Mongolia, but it is now clear to me that the true frontier is this double khangai zone. The root meaning of *khangai* is "that which satisfies a need or desire." *

For Mongols, a gobi is a stretch of land, usually low-lying and arid because it is low-lying, with a sparse vegetation of low-growing, tough, woody plants, good for camels, but also a thin scattering of what is called "white grass," which is also eaten by camels and is extremely nourishing for sheep and gazelles. In the bare patches the soil is a hard clay, or a sandy clay, or strewn with flat-flaked gravel. The color of the gravel may distinguish one gobi from another, as when one speaks of a "black gobi." Rain is rare and extremely irregular, and streams are correspondingly scarce. Livestock is watered mostly from wells, but the wells are often only a few feet deep, because the gobi zone is a long, shallow east-west trough, with subsoil water flowing from both its northern and southern rims toward the center. There are legends that this trough and the patches of sand dunes in it were created by the trampling of Chingis Khan's cavalry. What rain there is comes capriciously from clouds that are on their way from China toward higher country farther north; much of it from violent summer thunderstorms which may start a flash-flood in a dry gully and then not hit that patch of land again for several years.

Mongols do not think of "gobi" as "desert"; real desert they call *tsol gobi,* or simply *tsol.* Nor is gobi terrain forbidding. It is a pleasure to share in the lightening of hearts as a band of gobi-bred Mongols who have been

* See V. A. Kazakevich, Leningrad, *Sovremennaya mongol'skaya toponimika* ("Contemporary Mongolian Toponomy"), Academy of Sciences, "Works of the Mongolian Commission," No. 13, 1934. This talented scholar was a victim of the purges of the 1930's.

traveling through rich pasture where "the people live too close together"—in camps ten or twenty miles apart—feel the stride of their camels lengthening as the harder, barer country opens out ahead.

Altitude, temperature, and rain, then, have a great deal to do with the conditions under which a nomad lives. Rain in Mongolia, like temperature, has a wide range of variability. Between the years 1941 and 1960, the highest precipitation in Mongolia was 19.8 inches, in 1959, at Lamyn Khure, near the Siberian frontier; the lowest was 2.6 inches, in 1957, at Dalan Dzadagad, in the gobi zone. Sain Shand, in the oil-bearing region which is also in the gobi zone, recorded a low of 3.4 inches in 1958 against a high of 8.1 inches in 1959. In this twenty-year period Ulan Bator recorded 7.6 inches in 1941, almost a third of it in August and only a fraction of an inch in December. In 1960 it had almost 10 inches, the highest in July and the lowest in November.

Wheat is adaptable to wide differences of rainfall and temperature. In the United States, in Kansas and North Dakota and South Dakota, it is considered that wheat-growing is a gamble if the rainfall is under about 18 to 20 inches; but much depends on whether snow lies on the ground during the winter, conserving moisture in the soil, and on whether the rainy season coincides well with the growing season. A lot of the land that is newly being farmed in Mongolia has a thin topsoil, and it looked to me in danger of both gullying and sheet erosion under heavy rain, which increases the danger of "dust-bowl" formation in dry years with high winds. The Mongols insist, however, that they have taken the best Russian scientific advice, and that everything will be all right. It may be that by various devices, such as resting

a field after a harvest and not ploughing it again for two
or three years, the Mongols will be able to make farming
a more important adjunct to livestock-raising. At present—as often happens when marginal virgin lands are
first ploughed (I have seen this happen on Inner Mongolian land colonized by Chinese)—they are being very
successful. In 1961, for the first time in recorded history,
Mongolia had surplus grain to export.

3

Nomads and Their History

THE DATA in the last chapter make it clear why farming has always been much less important in Mongolia than pastoral nomadism. But this raises the question: "Just what is nomadism?" Many people still think of nomads as loosely organized tribes wandering about indefinitely, guided by the luck of the year's rain or lack of rain in their search for pastures, and from time to time gathering together in "hordes" when a succession of bad years forces them to try to conquer the pastures of other nomads, or to invade the lands of settled peoples. This notion is bolstered by tags and phrases that have become conventional, and stand in the way of fresh thinking. Gibbon, in his *Decline and Fall of the Roman Empire,* wrote of nomads in general that "The connection between the people and their territory is of so frail a texture that it may be broken by the slightest accident. The camp, and not the soil, is the native country of the genuine Tartar"; and the Chinese for centuries have described the nomads of Mongolia as "following grass and water"—with the implication that any grass, any water, is as good as any other grass or water.

The truth is the other way around. Nomadic life requires tight organization, technically skilled division of labor to cover a wide spread of activities, close gradation of responsibility and authority, precise legal concepts of territory—what land belongs to which tribe.

All through Central Asia winter pasture has always been the determining factor for the size of herds. Travelers and officials—the old Chinese and Manchu officials and the old Tsarist Russian officials—usually traveled through the pastures in summer, and they often wondered why the flocks and herds were not even larger. The reason was that there were not nearly enough good winter pastures. Of course, this could have been modified by supplementary agriculture to provide extra winter feed, and there was a certain amount of this kind of agriculture (more among the Kazakhs and Kirghiz than among the Mongols), but there never was as much of it as was needed, for the same old reason: the control of the society by its princes and chiefs was based on mobile herding; the immobilization of too many people, to attend to agriculture, would have upset the system.

Unless you have lived the life of the nomad all through the cycle of the year, it is difficult to realize how many technical factors are involved in bringing the livestock through the winter. If you must depend on winter grazing there must be both shelter and exposure. Horses can paw down through the snow to find the grass, and yaks can do this better than cows, but other livestock must have exposed areas where the wind blows off the snow. At the same time there must also be areas of shelter from the wind (except for yaks and camels), otherwise they will not be able to survive the spells of extreme cold. There is also the *dzud* (pronounced, in an approximate American manner, *dzawt*). This word means, basically, "lack of grazing," or "inability to graze," and it is used in many compound forms to indicate, for example, shortage of grazing when there is too much snow for the stock to get down to the pasturage, or not enough snow to serve as a substitute for water in a dry winter pasture, or the trampling flat of the herbage, so that it cannot be grazed, when for one reason or another too many animals have had to be concentrated on too small a pasture. This is called, picturesquely, the "hoof *dzud*." By far the commonest and most catastrophic *dzud*, however, occurs when there has been an unseasonable thaw followed by a sudden re-freeze. The herbage then becomes sheathed in a film of ice, the animals cannot graze, and in a few days may die off by the thousand or even the hundred thousand, bringing on a disaster comparable to that wrought by a total drought or torrential rains and the bursting of the banks of great rivers in monsoon Asia.

Though secondary to shortage of winter pasture, contagious and infectious cattle diseases were also a major factor in keeping down the size of the herds. Vaccination against cattle diseases was opposed by the lamas, and one traveler wrote in 1926 of a district where 75 per cent of the horned cattle perished in a few weeks.

Nomadic societies have survived these disasters for many centuries; one reason being that reduced herds, given one or two good seasons after the disaster, multiply and recover faster than fields baked by drought or covered with sand and silt by a flood. Survival, however, is quite a different thing from mastering the problem. That is something that can only be done by diversifying the economy, which means changing the society. Short of this, there are only mitigating measures, the most important of which is insurance by means of a primitive kind of co-operation. No disaster of either disease or weather affects all kinds of livestock equally. Therefore, in a region of considerable climatic diversity, like Mongolia, it is an insurance to own more than one kind of stock. But sheep, goats, cows, yaks, camels, and horses do not flourish equally on the same kind of pasture. Thus there arose long ago a primitive form of co-operation. One camp takes the sheep belonging to several camps, another the cows belonging to several camps, and so on, and each picks out the pasture best suited to the animals it is herding. Under the old conditions, however, the benefits of this kind of co-operation were limited, the range of movement being smaller because a camp-family was kept closely attached to the noble or monastery to which it belonged. Many camps had to get along as best they could with mixed herds on the same pasture.

Nomadism, moreover, is not a primitive form of society but a rather late evolution. Farming and city-building peoples have always looked down on nomads as "primitive," it is true; but this does not mean that nomads have reciprocated by looking up to the city and the farm. Far from it. There is a strong tradition among nomads that they are people who have made themselves free from the drudgery of the peasant and the shut-in life of the city dweller. They have good historical arguments on their side. Sheep and goats, cows and yaks, horses and asses (which were domesticated before horses, and became the ancestors of donkeys), and even the camel, were all domesticated by men who already knew about farming—not by primitive hunters who had thought things over and decided to breed animals instead of hunting them. The ancestors of the nomads—Arabs as well as Turks and Mongols—were men who decided to use these animals in order to break away from poverty-stricken farming into a more secure life as herdsmen.

Of course this was a choice that only certain people could make, under certain conditions. Perhaps 10,000 or 8000 years ago, in the neolithic age, in that zone of the Old World from the Mediterranean to the Pacific that is drier than the tropics and not so heavily forested as mid-Siberia and North Asia, men were living by a mixture of hunting, fishing, digging roots, gathering berries and wild fruit, and stripping the edible seeds of certain grasses, the ancestors of wheat, millet, barley, and oats. In time, they found that if some of the scattered seeds were left lying in favored spots—around springs and along the banks of small, slow, meandering streams—they would grow and there would be more than ever the next year; and that was how farming began, as a gradually emerging specialization within a mixed economy. Probably it was at first the work of the women, staying with the children in the favored localities, while the men ranged more widely, in hunting and, of course, in war. Men only became specialized farmers when farming became profitable enough to make it worth taking away from the women.

As farming prospered, men learned to farm on a larger scale, moving from limited fields around small oases and streams into bigger valleys and in time to the banks of the great rivers—the Nile, Tigris and Euphrates, Amu Darya and Syr Darya, Indus, and Yellow River. There, producing enough surplus to feed that part of the society that did not work at farming, they built the great

ancient city-and-farming states. A reverse development
then began. The great states reached back into the back
country, to demand taxes, tribute, and military and
labor service from the people still living there and still
farming in the older, more unskilled way; still depending in part on hunting and fishing and, by this time, also
herding considerable numbers of livestock. For it was
early in the age of mixed farming, hunting, and gathering that the pastoral animals had been domesticated.
Settlement around fields permanently or intermittently
cultivated had given time to build corrals in which to
keep, and so to "domesticate," young animals captured
by the hunters, by getting them used to contact with
men. The animals domesticated were those which could
be fed, during the time of adjustment, on the products
and by-products of farming. The capture of the young
animals in the first place may well have been to use
them as decoys in hunting. As men went along, they
discovered that they could "harvest" more in a year from
pastured animals than from wild game, and discovered
the by-products such as milk and cheese.

As Asian agriculture became more skilled, especially
with irrigation, the use of animals decreased, except for
the few used for ploughing. Agriculture fed plenty of
men, and men could be used for work on irrigation,
terracing, and all kinds of building. It was a shame to
use land to feed animals if it could be used to feed men.
It was therefore on the northern fringes of rich agriculture, from Syria to Manchuria, where much land could
not quite be used better to feed men than to feed animals, that the less successful farmers had the largest
number of animals at pasture to supplement their in-
adequate grain crops. It was this critical conjuncture, the

large number of animals and the poor agriculture on
the northern confines of the great ancient states of Asia,
that launched nomadism as an alternative way of life.
Because they were poor and because they were far away,
the demands of the tax-gatherer on these half-barbarous
people were especially cruel. Why not break away from
it all? Why not abandon the fields, take the animals,
and move away, to a zone still farther north where the
erratic rainfall made farming very risky, but was enough
to support a rich pasture?

This story is especially clear along the margin between
China and Mongolia—Inner Mongolia as well as Outer
Mongolia. It is the story of the Great Wall, marking off
the line beyond which a civilized state in China could
not expect to collect taxes and demand obedience. But
it is not the whole story. The critical period is in the
decades just before and just after 300 B.C. For centuries
before this period, the chronicles of the states of North
China (not yet unified as an empire) contain accounts of
wars against "barbarians." The record shows that these
wars were part of a steady Chinese expansion toward the
edge of what is now Inner Mongolia. These "barbarians"
were not pastoral nomads. There are several mentions of
the fact that they fought on foot, while the Chinese were
led by chariot-riding nobles. Then, along the Inner Mongolian frontier, in the period about 300 B.C., barbarians
of a new kind are mentioned—true nomads, who fought
as mounted archers.

The Chinese had in fact reached the limits of expansion in territory in which their kind of agriculturally
based power gave them the advantage. In the zone beyond, the barbarians who had been retreating before
them were beginning to abandon cultivation, rely on

their livestock, and become pastoral nomads—undoubtedly joining an older nomad society, also originating
along the margins of agriculture, which was already
there but had not yet been in direct contact with the
Chinese. For offensive warfare, to deal with these new
opponents, the Chinese adopted the nomad use of
mounted archers, and for defensive warfare developed
a special application of a technique long known to them
—the building of walls. In these decades each of the
northern states or kingdoms of China fortified its northern frontier. A century later, when China had been
unified by an internal conquest which created the first
true Chinese Empire—not by an invasion of foreign
conquerors—these sectional walls were linked up to form
the Great Wall.

The Great Wall of China is history's most absolute
statement of the idea of a frontier. "Beyond the Wall is
theirs. Everything on this side is ours." Yet in the lives
of men and the fate of dynasties all that the Great Wall
did was to establish the edge of an adjoining zone—the
Inner Mongolia of later centuries—merging northward
into Outer Mongolia, which stretched away to the unknown and as yet unnamed wildernesses of Siberia and
Inner Asia. The absoluteness of the frontier idea could
not be carried out because there was not in fact a confrontation of absolutely different societies. From the
neolithic age to the twentieth century there never was
a time when patches of agriculture did not exist here
and there in Mongolia, and nomadic life was further
modified by trade in both necessities and luxuries. Besides the wheat and millet grown in Mongolia, grain was
always imported. In the economy of the nomads it was
not exactly a necessity, but neither was it entirely a

luxury. Nomads could live well on a diet of meat, milk, and milk products, but the use of grain as a supplement helped to conserve the capital value of the live animals in the herds. A live sheep was a dividend, produced by the mating of its parents, but it was also new capital. Even a castrated sheep produced regular dividends in wool: but to butcher a sheep was to realize and consume its capital value, terminating its productivity.

Because agriculture and trade with agricultural countries were never eliminated from nomadic life, they never ceased to operate as modifiers of the nomadic economy and the political and military structures built on it. They were factors which interacted with the factors of mobility and dispersion in nomadic life. While it is true, as I have said above, that nomads migrate (in times of peace) only within their own territories, according to well-understood principles of the ownership of the territory by the political unit and rights of use by family units, it is also true that mobility is an essential principle of nomadism. Its importance is most sharply illustrated by the conditions of warfare. When a peasant population fled to escape from invaders, its manpower at once became unproductive, and it remained unproductive until it found new land or new occupations; but a nomadic tribe, if it retreated, took its herds along with it, and remained in production—even if the production was harried and diminished.

An opposite trend began, however, when a leader of nomadic warriors won a strong political and military position by skilled use of his mobile following. He could never refuse to exploit this position by acquiring agricultural, commercial, and even urban interests. More than his own cupidity or taste for luxury was involved;

he had also to reward faithful lieutenants, in order to
keep them loyal. This explains why the literature of
nomadic peoples, and of dynasties of nomadic origin
ruling in settled lands, is full of eulogies of the superior
virtues of the nomad as a man, while the history of
powerful nomadic rulers and dynasties of nomadic origin
is full of agriculture, trade, and cities. It was not only
that some nomads moved into conquered lands and
ceased to be nomads; powerful rulers who remained in
the land of pastures built cities in which to live more
luxuriously, and to feed the cities imported peasants
from China and the oases of Central Asia. Karakoram,
capital of Mongolia in the thirteenth and fourteenth
centuries, built by Ugedei, son of Chingis Khan, was a
city of this kind—a center for merchants and artisans,
with rich fields in sight of its walls, irrigated with water
from the Orkhon River. This irrigation is being revived
today: a sluice from the river feeds water into the tur-
bines of a hydroelectric station (part of the Chinese
program of aid to Mongolia), and the water is then distributed through irrigation canals. Karakoram is not an
exception. Traces of both rainfall and irrigated agriculture are normal near the many ruins of smaller cities in
Mongolia, and even the ruins of isolated fortresses around
which a city never clustered.

Then why are the ruins ruins? Why did the cities not
stay alive? Written history and archaeology give the
answer over and over again. The nomads closest to these
centers became less nomadic and less mobile, but the
land was huge and in both the drier and the colder pastures which agriculture did not penetrate, the nomadic
economy and the nomadic mobility were little modified.
There might be no war for a generation or two, but war

always returned, and when it did, the advantage reverted to those chiefs and warriors whose families and property were as mobile as the army itself.

There was one consequence of this alternation between the more and the less mobile phases that has never yet been studied by a military or social historian: the corresponding alternation between elite, aristocratic, heavy-armed cavalry in small numbers and the light cavalry of mounted archers who represented a total mobilization of the manpower of a tribe or people, as in the time of Chingis Khan. The small Mongolian horse, grazing entirely on the open range with no barns and no supplementary grain feed, is amazingly tough. It can carry a man more than a hundred miles in a day— but not the next day; it must have a few days to graze and rest. Chingis Khan handled this problem by gearing his army to the average horse. His cavalry were accompanied by herds of remounts, which were treated like the standardized, interchangeable parts of a machine. There was no great difference between today's horse and tomorrow's horse: both were called on only for average performance.

At the other end of the scale of alternation were the Orkhon Turks who occupied central and western Mongolia in the Middle Ages, and who reached their greatest power in the seventh and eighth centuries. Their elite warriors were heavy-armed nobles, a kind of chivalry. Both the horse and his noble rider wore defensive armor, and to carry this extra weight a bigger, stronger horse was needed. The right kind of horse was provided as much by feeding as by breeding—and probably also by the use of sheltered stables in winter. The growth of the ordinary Mongolian horse is stunted by the bitter winters.

It is probable that most of the ordinary tribesmen of the Orkhon Turks were truly nomadic; but the nobles, in order to breed their special horses, had to live near their agricultural center in the Orkhon valley. They thus made themselves less mobile, and the Chinese of the great T'ang dynasty were eventually able to pin them down and defeat them. The T'ang Chinese, incidentally, also used Turkish cavalry, recruited among semi-nomadic Turks who had settled within the Great Wall, in North China; they probably also rode strong, grain-fed horses.

All nomads are widely dispersed, as compared with farmers, but some nomads are more widely dispersed than others, depending on the region and the kind of livestock pastured. Broadly speaking, the northeastern plains are the best pasture for cows; in the past, the ox-cart was used here more than the camel caravan. The Gobi territory is the homeland of the camel, but in the southwest, in the Gobi-Altai region, camels are used in quite rough, hilly country. A sand-bred camel has large, round, but thinly padded hoofs; a hill-bred camel has smaller but more thickly padded hoofs. A hill-bred camel does better in the sand than a sand-bred camel does in the hills, where his thin pads are easily blistered by stony surfaces.

In the northwest, a difference of 500 to 1000 feet in altitude can be critical in determining between cow pasture and yak pasture. Yaks can get down through quite thick snow to find grazing, while cows are baffled by a rather thin snow-cover. The yak gives about as much milk as the cow (depending on pasture), but with a much higher butter-fat content. The differences between yak territory and cow territory, and between yak qualities and cow qualities, are bridged by a yak-cow cross, the *khainag.* This cross does well on both the higher and the lower pastures; it gives more milk than the yak, with more butter fat than the cow. The genetic balance of this animal, however, is peculiar; in the second generation it produces a very scraggly animal. A permanent mixed breed has therefore never become established; instead, the khainag is crossed back to one or the other parent stock.

In such back-crossing, the half-bred yak-cow bull is regarded as sterile, the half-bred yak-cow cow as fertile. There are specific terms for these crosses. If the sire is a yak and the mother a cow, the cross is called a "water-khainag," if the sire is a domestic bull and the mother a yak-cow, the cross is called a "sun-khainag." For the Mongols, the decision to castrate surplus bull-calves, full-bred or half-bred, is quite simple. Unlike the European or American, they are not worried about fattening calves to slaughter for veal. With plenty of pasture, why slaughter the animal too young? On the contrary, they still need thousands of oxen to pull carts. Therefore the castrated bull-calf is allowed to grow to full size as a working ox.

Horses, sheep, and goats are the universal animals, found in every part of Mongolia but not in uniform quality. The handsomest and fastest horses come from the eastern half of the northern frontier, near Siberia. They have the build of a small horse, while other Mongol horses have a more stubby, heavy-necked, pony-like build. To every horse, however, his own homeland; a mountain-bred horse is best in the mountains, a sand-bred horse in the sands. For some reason, crosses with the Anglo-Don and other Russian varieties seem always to produce a hard-gaited animal. The Mongols do not like a hard, pounding trot but a fast, shuffling, smooth gait, the pattern of which is like a very much accelerated walk.

Goats are traditionally the least-valued Mongol livestock. The Mongols like fat meat, and goats have much less fat than sheep; also, sheepskins with the fleece on make much better winter gowns than goatskins, and sheep's wool makes a much stronger felt than camel hair. The most valuable product of the goat is one that has always been little used by the Mongols but is a high-priced export: it is "cashmere," the soft underwool which is not shorn but combed out from the outer covering of goat-hair. The quantity and quality of Mongolian cashmere are being improved by cross-breeding.

There are several breeds of Mongolian sheep, adapted to all kinds of pastures—from the high and cold to the low and sandy. While the horse has always been the noble animal, the sheep is economically indispensable to the old nomadic life. It is the only animal that supplies all the basic needs: food, clothing, housing, fuel. Besides meat, it provides milk for drinking and for making cheese. The hide with the fleece on makes the best heavy winter gown. The wool, matted into felt, covers the *ger,* the round, domed Mongol tent. (Nowadays, although the inner covering of the tent is still felt, which is the best insulator, the outer covering is normally of heavy white canvas, which sheds water well and absorbs less dust than felt.) When sheep are penned at night, they trample the dung that they drop. It gradually builds up in thickness, until it can be spaded out in rectangular bricks and burned as fuel. It makes a very hot fire, but its smoke is very irritating to the eyes. The best dung-fuel is cow dung; the next best is camel dung. The most obvious mark of the different breeds or strains of the Mongolian sheep is the size of the tail, which varies from a small, goat-sized tail to a huge mass of fat weighing forty pounds or more.

One of the great successes of experimental cross-breeding in Mongolia has been the establishment of a new breed of sheep, the "Orkhon." It has almost all the hardiness of the native breeds and a finer, longer staple of wool, good for modern machine-made textiles. It also produces a good mutton. It is an oddity of Central Asian history, which I cannot explain, that the Turkish-speaking peoples have always made woolen textiles, while the Mongols until recently never did.

The pasturing of all these animals is an art, which includes skills of a kind that one might call folk science: a way of making use of the environment that combines a great deal of knowledge, coming from shrewd observation, with a certain amount of harmful supersitition. When preparing to go to Mongolia after an absence of so many years, I knew that I ought to refresh my knowledge of the language with new words and expressions for new things and ideas. Looking over my shelves I found a book called *Advice to Herdsmen,* which I had bought in Poland several years before but not yet read. I took it along and worked hard on it on the sea voyage to Denmark, and the train journey from Denmark to Mongolia. I found it a wonderful book, written in the most difficult style of all, requiring a real master: the everyday spoken language of the people, but used with literary distinction, at once firm and delicate. The author was clearly a man who knew the old life and the old arts, but also a judicious believer in improvements and scientific innovations. He wrote in a way to win the con-

fidence of old-fashioned herdsmen by showing them that
he was at home in their life, and by winning their confidence to persuade them to go along with him on new
ideas. Many passages of this book, if translated, would
be of absorbing interest to Americans who handle livestock on the open range.

When we got to Mongolia I mentioned this book to
a Mongol friend. "Why, of course," he said, "that's
Sambuu, our President. Everybody knows he knows his
stuff, and even people who no longer handle cattle admire
his writing." The President, in Mongolia as in other
Communist-ruled countries, is the head of the executive
government, but not of the Party, which determines
policy. Mr. Sambuu, I am told, is now working on a
history of religion in Mongolia. It ought to be quite a
book.

Some of the problems of the art and practice of pas-
toralism are easy to understand. I have already mentioned that there is a critical altitude above which it
becomes more profitable to herd yaks than cows. Then
there is the fact that there is never such a thing as a pasture on which only one kind of grass grows. There is
always a mixture—the mixture varies according to rainfall and temperature—and out of the mixture some animals prefer some grasses and other animals prefer other
grasses. Sheep eat a larger variety of grasses than horses
or cows, but if you keep sheep too long on a good sheep
pasture they turn it into a bad sheep pasture—because
they crop short the grasses they prefer, which gives the
other grasses a chance to seed and spread, displacing the
good sheep grasses. There are also grasses which at an
early stage of their growth are good for one animal or
another, but not at a later stage. Then there is the fact

that sheep crop the pasture so close that horses and cows, which like to bite at taller tufts of herbage, have a poor time of it if they are put on pasture that has been freshly grazed by sheep. This is only a sampling of problems. There are others, like the pasturing of young animals apart from older animals of the same kind.

Sambuu, in the book I have referred to, gives a great many examples: On khangai pasture, when handling cows, the best combination for supervision, grazing, and watering is a herd of 30 for cows who are expected to calve within six weeks and cows with calves up to six months old; 45 for cows at earlier stages of pregnancy, and cows with calves more than six months old; 150 for young cattle a full year old and on through their second and third years, and for barren cows. These figures change for other kinds of pasture and other kinds of animal. Camels can be handled in larger herds on poor gobi grazing than on rich pasture, but all other animals ought to be herded in larger numbers on good pasture, smaller numbers on poor pasture.

These considerations mean that the adept herdsman must rotate the use of pasture by different kinds of live-stock—which brings him up against logistics. When moving a herd from one grazing ground to another both the speed of movement and the distance moved in a day are different for different animals, if they are to be kept in good condition; moreover, speed and distance are different for the same animals at different seasons of the year. For the families accompanying the animals these requirements impose a shifting pattern of dispersal and concentration: how many families may camp together at what season of the year, and how far away from the next camp they may be. The always-present need to do what is best for the animals also has both an economic and a social effect on the human society. For the owner of livestock, as for the capitalist investor, it is wise to diversify. To own several kinds of animal is an insurance against the kind of disaster that might kill off most of the cows but spare most of the sheep. But a family with only a few head of cattle cannot meet both this requirement and the requirement that different herds be pastured separately. Out of such needs, grew the primitive co-operation already mentioned: "You take my cows and your cows and his cows and pasture over there, and I'll take your sheep and his sheep and my sheep, and pasture here"— and so on.

For the sake of simplicity, I have been writing as if every Mongol were an owner; but there is a higher degree of complication to be taken into account. Throughout their history, the Mongols were a people of nobles and commoners, and sometimes also of slaves and war captives, and of subordinate tribes which, without being enslaved, lived under the protection and at the orders of stronger tribes. Poor families often owned no cattle at all, but pastured the herds of nobles, the rich, or the tribal chief or lord; others, who did own livestock, paid tribute to those above them. It was therefore the ruling families, whose executive head was the chief or prince of the tribe, who dominated the whole complex—the allocation of pastures and the assignment of families to this duty and that.

What about nomadic life as a whole? The alternation between periods when cities were built and agriculture encouraged and periods in which, in order to secure power in the shortest time, the nomad was encouraged to move helps to explain many peculiarities of Mongol tradition and custom. The Mongols have never been breeders of pigs and chickens. Even where good water could be reached at a depth of a few feet, they did not dig nearly as many wells as were needed to shorten migrations between one pasture and another. Only in the last few years have the Mongols begun to overcome their prejudices against such foods as fish, pork, and the meat and eggs of birds. Why such prejudices, and such neglect of profitable opportunities? I think the answer is bound up with the last cycle of nomadism, only partly modified, since the seventeenth century, by the building of monasteries and the development of a few trading centers.

The man who digs a well has a claim to it, and might like to linger near it while others move on: pigs cannot be herded in the open in Mongolia; chickens cannot be moved about; the man who says "No, I want to stay here; it is the fishing season," or "it is the season of migrating wildfowl," is not available for assignment to routine herding duties, and might acquire a kind of economic independence outside the established order. All such things went against the interest of those who mobilized, directed and exacted tribute from the nomadic life.

What a society in which to launch a revolution guided by Marxism, with its proletarian, strongly urban inspiration! No wonder strange things have happened in Mongolia in the last forty years.

4

Autonomous Mongolia: The Years of Frustration

THE YEAR 1961 was celebrated as the fortieth anniversary of the campaigns of 1921 and the proclamation of a new Provisional Government in Mongolia. It happened to be also the fiftieth anniversary of 1911, when the Mongols had revolted against the Manchu Empire, founded their Autonomous Government, and done their best to separate themselves from China. The celebration of 1921, without celebrating 1911, means that in the official view 1911 had been only the false dawn of an old-fashioned nationalistic revolution. True revolution had begun only in 1921.

What the Mongols had wanted in 1911 was complete independence. By their rebellion against the Manchu Empire they were trying to affirm that the link between Mongolia and China was artificial. The Manchus in the seventeenth century had separately conquered first China and then Mongolia. Therefore, when the Manchus fell, the link was broken. China was free to become a republic and Mongolia to go its own way.

If the world had stood by and let the Mongols have freedom, as freedom was understood in 1911, they would have foundered. The Mongols of that day simply did not have the resources, the organization, or the individual men of ability to administer an independent state. But what did happen was that the heads of the religious hierarchy and the nobility turned immediately to Tsarist Russia for protection of their country and support of their own positions within the country.

Tsarist Russia, however, preferred to support Mongolia only to the extent of autonomy—not independence. The period was one of standstill arrangements between Russia, Japan, and Britain. Following the Russo-Japanese War of 1904-05 Russia and Japan had negotiated several secret treaties (since published) defining the extent to which Japan had displaced Russia from Manchuria and indicating (though naming only "the meridian of Peking") the eastern frontier of Mongolia as the zone separating Russian and Japanese interests. As part of the same general trend of policy, an Anglo-Russian Convention was signed in 1907 allocating Mongolia to Russia and Tibet to Britain as spheres of interest.

There is a distinction to be made in all this between different imperialisms. Japan was preparing the way for further expansion. Russia and Britain were abandoning their ambitions for annexation of Chinese territory and trying to terminate their rivalry with each other. They were buffering their agreed frontiers. Britain regarded Tibet, and Russia regarded Mongolia, as regions which belonged to China but were not really parts of China, because the Tibetans and Mongols were not Chinese. They would neither go all the way in supporting the Tibetan and Mongol claim that the Manchu throne had been the only link between China, Mongolia, and Tibet, nor all the way in admitting the Chinese claim that Mongolia and Tibet were "integral" parts of China. This enabled them to support the Tibetans and Mongols, and make them look to Britain and Russia for continuing support, without taking the responsibility of forcing China to admit complete Tibetan and Mongol independence.

Even in the weakness and confusion of the collapsing Manchu dynasty and the first years of the Republic, the Chinese did their best to stake out claims for the long future by stubborn defense at the negotiating table, by such devices as granting laudatory titles to Mongol and Tibetan leaders, by occasional military expeditions, and by colonizing with Chinese settlers in frontier regions. A belt of Chinese farming was established in northern Mongolia, near the Siberian frontier and out of contact with the gradual, continuous-spread colonization of Chinese in Inner Mongolia.

The frontier peoples also responded in their own way to these developments. Contrary to what usually happens in periods of imperialism, both the Tibetans and the Mongols wanted more, not less, British and Russian intervention in their countries. This attitude was of the greatest importance in the case of the Mongols: it preconditioned their minds for the appeal to Soviet Russia to enter their country in 1921. This preconditioning may be described as the psychological feeling that "the Chinese (and later the Japanese) are always wanting to push in too far; the Russians are always having to be persuaded to come in far enough."

What Tsarist Russia supported in Mongolia from 1911 until its own collapse in 1917 was a typical protectorate.

With Manchu authority gone, none of the great regional nobles could be promoted to act as Head of State, because that would have made his peers jealous. Therefore, this new office was assigned to the most eminent religious figure in the country, the Jebtsundamba Hutukhtu or "Living Buddha of Urga." As he was a Tibetan by birth, he was not even related to any of the noble families. He took the title of Kaghan and the reign style of "Elevated by All"—an historical fiction, suggesting that he had been recognized by the acclamation of the chiefs and warriors, in the ancient tribal tradition. As a lama he was supposed to be celibate, but in his new secular capacity his concubine was also officially given a title, making her a sort of queen. This anomaly did not bother anyone any more than comparable goings-on bothered people in Europe in the days of the Medici Popes.

At the beginning of this period there was some dis-agreement between the new government of Mongolia and its Russian protectors on the subject of Inner Mongolia, where a number of rebellions against the new Chinese Republic broke out. The rebels were clamoring for union with Outer Mongolia, and the Living Buddha was in favor of welcoming them, though he was not equally in favor of some of their leaders. He did not want new men coming in from the fringes and, in the name of their own kind of nationalism, claiming an ascendancy in "his" Outer Mongolia. Not knowing of the secret spheres-of-influence agreements between Russia and Japan, he even tried to approach the Japanese to ask for their support, but the Japanese evaded these overtures, and the Russians, when they learned of them, strongly disapproved. Apart from this, the Russo-Mongol relationship soon settled into the usual protectorate pattern:

some loans, a bank, tariff agreements favoring Russian
trade, the training of a small army under Russian instructors, and the installation of some Russian advisers,
including a financial adviser—who later went over to the
revolutionary side and in time became a member of
the Soviet Academy of Sciences, as a scholar in the Mongol language and literature.

Ministries and a Cabinet were formed, providing an
area in which powerful nobles and ecclesiastical officials
competed in cliques for the distribution of power, privilege, and handsome personal grants in money. There
was no such thing as a political party to give a voice to
people who were not already powerful in either the
nobility or the church. More than anything else, an
almost incredible ignorance of economics revealed the
unreadiness of the Mongols for life as a nation. There
was no middle class. The merchants and small traders
had almost all been Chinese, although Russian trade had
begun to make inroads. The artisans were also mostly
Chinese, although a few Mongols, including artisan-
monks, were skilled workers in wood, leather, and
metals. The Chinese grip was made tighter by the completely "feudal" attitude toward money of the upper-
class Mongols. "Money? Oh, that's something you get
from money-lenders; and while we're at it, we might as
well let them keep the accounts."

To live among Mongols for a while brings a new real-
ization of how the minds of Western men were transformed by the important historical period of the rise of
the middle classes, between the decline of feudalism and
the coming of industrialism. Under Communism, as before Communism, a Mongol does not measure status and
self-esteem in account-keeping, money-reckoning terms,

but by the respect which the community gives him if it thinks he "is doing an important job, is somebody who matters."

As merchants, money-lenders, managers, contractors, and transportation agents, the Chinese, though aliens, worked within the very entrails of the Mongol society. There was one Chinese firm—this figure is so frequently cited in the literature that it must be the biggest available figure—that used to drive out of Mongolia every year 70,000 horses and a half a million sheep, collected as payments against loans and interest. There were massacres of Chinese in western Mongolia in 1911, after which the fear of violence all over the country made thousands flee back to China. The supply and distribution of trade goods suffered, and economic hardships were increased in a country already politically restive— but when revolution came, it came to a society that had neither a proletariat nor a middle class, a setting unique in the history of Communist-led revolutions.

There had been risings, rebellions, and military mutinies in Mongolia before, but never a true revolution. There was a Mongol equivalent of the Chinese peasant rebellion, in which tenants rose against their landlords and fought against the government only when the government intervened on the side of the landlords. The Mongol form was the rebellion of the *arat* (modern spelling, *ard*), the "commoners" who were the subjects of princes and of monastic domains, and who, in addition to paying tribute in cash or livestock, were liable to many feudal services. There lingered among the people the memory of an ancient time in which the "tribe" had been essentially an organization of the men of fighting age, and the "prince" a war chief whose claim to his

position was partly by heredity, but had also to be sanc-
tioned by the consent of the warriors; for, if the position
had been purely by heredity, without such a sanction,
it could not be guaranteed that the new chief would be
a good leader in war. Because of this lingering tradition,
Mongol rebellion against a prince sometimes was limited
by the demand that the prince be replaced by someone
better, from the same family. The characteristic form of
rebellious organization was the *duguilang* ("that which
is in a circle"); those who joined signed their names in
a circle or "ring," so that if the organization were discovered, no "ringleader" could be identified.

There had been rebellions of this kind in both Inner
and Outer Mongolia for several decades, with increasing
frequency. Those of Inner Mongolia were usually complicated by the factor of encroaching Chinese colonization; those of Outer Mongolia were not; they were rebellions within the society itself, against the abuses
which were making the society unbearable, and they
give us a clear idea of the pressures that were building
up from a rebellion-intensity to a revolution-intensity.
Some of the lesser nobility began to join the rebellions—
a symptom which showed that the ruling class was no
longer able to take care of its own. The younger son or
nephew of a great noble, not standing in the direct line
of succession, could no longer take it for granted that the
path of the nobility was his own path to success and standing. Lucrative appointments were harder and harder to
get, and family revenues were shrinking. The discontented young noble who was also a bold man and felt
that he had the gift of leadership was increasingly
tempted to make a bid for the leadership of the rebellious commoners. (Sometimes the acceptance of this

leadership was disastrous for the commoners, if the noble was a man who could be bought back to the side of the old order by offers to make amends for the way in which he had been neglected.)

The Mongol herdsman had many onerous duties. He had to herd his lord's cattle; provide his lord not only with milk, cheese, and (especially in summer) fermented mare's milk, but hides and the dressed skins of sheep and lambs (with the wool on); was liable for service at the lord's headquarters; had to gather cow dung for fuel; and attend on his lord's journeys. In addition, there were duties to the state which, according to the usages of feudalism, were passed on down through the nobles to their subjects. The herdsman was subject to military duty. There was also a double system of communications throughout the country—the post-stations—for carrying official messages and for forwarding official travelers on their way. This system, much admired by Europeans since the Middle Ages, was hated by the Mongols. Horses had to be provided—and the lord would never provide a horse of his own, as long as he had a subject who owned a horse. Somebody had to ride with the message, or to escort the traveler, from one station to the next, and to bring back the horses—and whoever heard of a noble discharging this duty? Related to this system was the requirement for "tethered horses"—horses which had to be kept ready at national and regional points in case they needed to be ridden on official duty. Here again the lord would never provide a horse, as long as he had a subject who owned one.

These requirements, however, introduce another symptom of crisis—flight, as a variant of rebellion or in combination with rebellion. The herdsman was not a

land-bound peasant. Almost all the duties that were required of him had something to do with four-footed
animals. Unlike the peasant, who if he fled from oppression had to abandon the field which was his only source
of food, the herdsman could, in fleeing, take with him
some of the animals—his own or his lord's—which he
would need to keep himself alive. Moreover, in many
regions of Outer Mongolia—much more than Inner
Mongolia—it was possible to keep alive by hunting.
There is much reference in the sources to *berdan* and
vintov—Mongol versions of the names of obsolete Russian Army muskets and rifles—which had filtered into
Mongolia from Siberia. The wide-open spaces of Outer
Mongolia were much roomier than those of Inner Mongolia, cramped by Chinese colonization. Gun in hand,
and lifting with him a few animals—his own or his
lord's—the Mongol could go "over the hill" and survive;
perhaps in poverty, but better the poverty of a free man,
than that of a serf. I have always felt that Marxist writers
have neglected this difference, in rebellion, between the
mobile herdsman and the land-bound peasant.

There are references in the Mongolian State Archives
to the acuteness of this problem: it intensified both the
social and the economic crisis. By bearing down too hard
on those who supported them in a declining economy,
the ruling classes forced some into rebellion, some into
flight. Both those who fled and those who rebelled
diminished the economic base of the aristocracy and the
monasteries which ruled quasi-feudal domains. By doing
so they forced the ruling classes to exploit even more
cruelly those who remained, and thus to increase both
rebellion and flight.

Be that as it may, the sparks that made the smoldering

fire of rebellion burst into the searing flame of revolution came from outside the country. I suspect that more often than not in the history of revolutions the building up of pressures to detonation point is internal, and the detonating spark external, and that one of the most responsible tasks of the historian is to distinguish between the tinder and the spark.

In the case of Mongolia, the sparks began to fly when Tsarist Russia was defeated by the Kaiser's Germany in the First World War. A feudal structure of society requires a sovereign-patron at the apex, and as far as the structure is concerned, the sovereign may be either benign or malign. The Manchus had begun by being malign, in destroying the regional sovereignties of Inner and Outer Mongolia. They had shifted toward an Inner Mongolian policy that on the whole continued to be malign, in supporting Chinese colonizing encroachment, but an Outer Mongolian policy that was up to the last moment benign (from the feudal point of view) in working through the ecclesiastical and secular hierarchy of privileges. In Outer Mongolia, when the Manchu Emperor had fallen off the top of the pyramid, the Russian Tsar had moved over to sit in his place. When the Tsar in turn fell off the top, in 1917, who or what was to come next?

During the First World War Japan was free to follow an ambivalent imperialist line. It was an ally of Britain, and later the United States, but at the same time it worked against its Western allies to create for itself a special position in China by controlling corrupt Chinese politicians through political loans, and by many other measures. One of the instruments of Japanese policy was a group of politicians and war lords known as the Anfu

Clique, and one of the clique was General Hsü Shu-tseng, called "Little" Hsü, to distinguish him from another Hsü.

In 1918, taking advantage of the fall of the Tsarist regime, Japan extended its operations to Mongolia. From Manchuria, and the corner where the frontiers of Manchuria, Mongolia, and Siberia join, Japan operated through anti-Bolshevik Russians such as the Siberian Cossack Ataman Semenov, and also through anti-Chinese Mongols and anti-Russian Buryats. In the corner territory just mentioned lies the Manchurian region of Barga, inhabited by Mongols. Following the 1911 Revolution these Mongols had fought hard to break away from China and join Autonomous Outer Mongolia, but had been frustrated by Tsarist Russia's refusal to accept a "Pan-Mongolian" movement. Japan now revived the "Greater Mongolia" slogan, which nicely fitted the design of a zone of imperialist control expanded from Japan's already strong position in Manchuria to take in Mongolia and part of Siberia. This part of the Japanese plan of operations was both anti-Chinese and anti-Mongol, since it aimed at detaching Mongolia from China and then controlling it through Japan's own Mongol nominees.

At the same time, however, the Japanese co-ordinated this eastern approach to Mongolia through Manchuria with a southern approach from Peking, which was then in the hands of Japan's war-lord agents, the Anfu Clique, and "Little" Hsü was sent up to Mongolia with a military expedition. The Living Buddha's government, frightened by the tide of Bolshevik revolution that was beginning to flow through Siberia and hesitating between the pressures from the east and south, allowed this force to enter the country and garrison the capital, Urga.* In this adventure "Little" Hsü was both carrying out Japanese policy and pursuing a personal aim typical of the war lords of that time—the acquisition of an additional territory to plunder. As for the Mongols themselves, even the Living Buddha recoiled from the idea of letting his government and his country be taken over by "Greater Mongolia" Buryat and Inner Mongolian nationalists, in spite of the fact that the Inner Mongolian spokesmen were as conservative as he was and also the fact that, for a while after 1911, he had wanted to add some Inner Mongolian territory to his own country.

In this he represented the main line of tradition among the Mongols of Outer Mongolia, who for some centuries have considered the Buryats and the Mongols of Inner Mongolia to be "less Mongol" than they are, or at least "Mongol in a different way." The Manchus had approached through Inner Mongolia, and used Inner Mongolian troops, to conquer Outer Mongolia and add it to their empire, and ever since the idea of unifying all the Mongols has been examined with suspicion by the Mongols of Outer Mongolia, who have always been wary of anybody from outside who wanted to do the unifying. Westerners, who tend to think that if nationalism is good

* The explanation of the name Urga (now Ulan Bator) is interesting. It is the Russian pronunciation of the Mongol word örgöö (old spelling, eruge), which is the name for the flap of felt which can be drawn over the smoke-hole at the top of the round, domed, Mongol felt tent. Used honorifically, it denotes not only the flap but the whole tent of an important person—as when one says "residence" instead of "home." Historically, the city of Urga grew up at the point where the Jebtsundamba Hutukhtu established his "residence." The modern name, Ulan Bator (Ulaan Baatar in the new spelling) is revolutionary; it means Red Hero.

then "greater" nationalism must be better, often fail to understand these distinctions in Mongol nationalism.

By the summer of 1919 the Chinese felt strong enough, with their garrison dominating Urga and with Japanese support in the background, to demand that the Living Buddha "voluntarily" sign a renunciation of Mongolia's autonomy and a recognition of complete Chinese sovereignty. They also demanded repayment of debts to Chinese, with accumulated interest. In western Mongolia, where the Chinese had suffered most in 1911-12, an indemnity of 50,000 camels was collected. There is confusion in the diplomatic and military history of this crisis. There were hard-line Chinese—the war lord—and soft-line Chinese—the representative of the Foreign Office. In the Mongolian Government, the high ecclesiastics took a weaker stand than the princes. In the "Parliament"—which I put in quotation marks because it was chosen rather than elected—the Lower Chamber rejected the ultimatum, but the Upper Chamber gave in. The Living Buddha managed not to sign the surrender document himself, but his five Cabinet Ministers signed it for him.

In the next year, 1920, there was a new crisis. "Little" Hsü, once in full control of Mongolia, had gone even further in the interests of Japanese policy and stationed some of his troops in Siberia, not far from the Mongolian frontier. Then he had gone back to Peking, leaving subordinates in charge, only to find that his war-lord group, the Anfu Clique, had lost control of the Chinese government, which passed temporarily into the hands of a war lord more favorable to Britain and America and therefore less favorable to Japan.

The Japanese then reverted to their other policy, that

of the "eastern approach," from Manchuria, and the "Greater Mongolia" slogan. Here the first instrument of their policy had been the Siberian Cossack Ataman Semenov, who is said to have been a Buryat on his mother's side. Calling himself for the time being a subordinate of Semenov's was the Baltic Baron Ungern-Sternberg, or Ungern von Sternberg, a pathological sadist who was soon to make himself infamous as the "Mad Baron." Since "Little" Hsü was no longer in power, the Japanese had no more use for his troops and allowed the Mad Baron to drive them out of Urga. Most of them were unable to make their way back to China, and soon the northern half of Mongolia and the entry into Siberia by the main trade route from Urga were swarming with bands of demoralized Chinese, living off the country, attacking helpless Mongol camps, and killing people because they were half crazy with fear themselves.

To these were added the depredations not only of Ungern-Sternberg's troops but those of Kasagrandi, Rezukin, and other minor anti-Bolshevik commanders retreating into Mongolia. The stories of some of the survivors of these detachments have been published, and in them the madness of fear crops up again and again.[*] One officer would shoot another in order to get control of his men, and when strangers came into sight men would shoot, assuming that strangers would be enemies, not friends. One book from these times, highly sensationalized, was published all over the world in many languages, but its author, too, was accused of having

[*] I. I. Serebrennikov, *Velikii otkhod* (*The Great Exodus*), Harbin, 1936.

abandoned comrades.* The worst of them all was the
Mad Baron. Of the Russians in Mongolia he killed every
Jew he could find, shot any other Russian he thought
might not be entirely one of his own men, and to maintain "discipline" among his troops would pick out men
here and there in the ranks and have them shot, just
"to encourage the others." He also had insane dreams of
uniting Mongols, Tibetans, Manchus—anybody who was
not Russian and not Chinese (since he himself was a
Balt, not a Russian)—to sweep the world with a conquest
more devastating than the wildest exterminations attrib-
uted (not always correctly) to Chingis Khan.

But in trying to write about the Mongols, not just
about people from outside who happened to be in Mongolia, the great question is, How did these crises affect
the Mongol people, the nation as a whole. Were they
so ignorant, politically so immature, so far below the
level that we call "civilized" that anybody with power
in his hand could come along, give orders, and expect
to be obeyed? A clear answer can be given, because the
Mongolian National Archives are full of documents
which make it possible to reconstruct exactly what went
on. A movement developed which was genuinely Mongol
and national, in that it was a response by Mongols to
Mongol problems. There was also, however, a strong
infusion of ideas coming from Russia—ideas about what
to do and how to do it. Not all of these ideas were Marxist, but from an early phase the Marxist influence was
ascendant. Furthermore, the data make it possible to
understand why the Chinese, in spite of the fact that
they too had been struggling through a long revolu-

* Ferdinand Ossendowski, *Beasts, Men and Gods*, New York,
1922.

tionary process, had so much less influence than the
Russians did on the way that Mongols thought and acted.
For a full decade, the ordinary Mongol had been getting poorer, more discontented, more disillusioned in
his discontent, and more willing to act radically. The
belief that "the big fellows always sell us out" had become an article of faith among the common people.
Among the "big fellows" they included not only most
of the princes but much of the ecclesiastical establishment. In Western countries, especially those where the
religious tradition is mainly Protestant, it is often insuf-
ficiently understood that a man can be both devoutly
religious and toughly anti-clerical. In Mongolia, where
monastic institutions owned territory, collected taxes,
and demanded labor services, the "idle monk," the
"hypocritical priest," and the "grasping abbot" were
stock figures of popular satire, as in medieval Europe.
It was perfectly consistent to say, "the Living Buddha
of that monastery over there is a very holy man, and
we must reverence him; but we are also entitled to hate
the guts of his administrators, who put the screws on us."

The people felt that every time there was a deal over
national autonomy, over debts to Chinese merchants,
over anything at all, there was also a sell-out. The big
fellows came out of it with new titles, emoluments, and
stipends. Then they turned around and wanted more
taxes and special contributions from the people to pay
for it all. They incited ordinary Mongols to massacre
and beat up Chinese merchants and money-lenders, and
burn their account books, but that just put the big
fellows in a position to say to the Chinese, later, "Well,
forget about my personal debt and I'll help you to collect
the rest."

The Mongols had a military tradition through which to express their discontent. Their legends, as Damdinsüren, one of Mongolia's great living scholars, has pointed out, are full of stories of the poor boy from nowhere who fought against the "bad" khan and made himself a "good" khan, a "khan of the people." There was hardly such a thing as a Mongol who could not ride; and because hunting was a part-time occupation all over the country, there were far more guns, even if not very good ones, and far more people who knew how to use them, than in rural China. With a horse between his knees and a gun in his hand, the Mongol was ready for action. And action there was. The most famous example was that of Ayush, a man of the western part of the country. From 1911 to 1917, he was a leader of rebels who refused to pay unjust usurious debts to Chinese, or bow their necks to oppression. He never controlled a large region or commanded a large number of men, but he held out long enough to become known and admired all over the country.

Where Mongols were in contact with Chinese, the conditions did not favor common action arising out of similar grievances. If the Chinese were a colonizing farmer, he might be miserably poor and cruelly exploited by his landlord, but he had been placed where he was by an official policy which favored the Chinese against the Mongol. There was a confrontation of hostility, but little contact. The Chinese was a grain-eater and did not drink milk, so he bought practically nothing from the Mongols for food. He worked as much as he could by hand, so he bought little livestock. He wore cotton clothes and quilted cotton in winter if he could, and so did not buy many sheepskins. Because contact was so limited, he almost never learned to speak Mongol. The setting favored the worst kind of nationalism, that of mutual contempt and dislike, not a union of the oppressed.*

If the Chinese were a merchant, a shopkeeper, or an artisan making trade-goods, everything depended on whether he was rich, making his money out of capital and interest, or a wage-earning clerk or artisan. Big merchants made deals with princes and monasteries, for whom they often acted as general agents, disposing of cattle, wool, and hides collected as tribute, and receiving guarantees for the collection of debts from commoners. They were Mongolia's middle class, its bourgeoisie—but because they were foreigners, the resentment against them was diverted from the channel of class conflict, which Marxists like to emphasize, into that of nationalist hatred, which Marxists deplore.

The wage-earning Chinese were different, in ways that are extremely interesting to the historian of society. There was a law on the books, dating from Manchu times and deriving from the Manchu policy of keeping Mongols and Chinese apart from each other, forbidding Chinese either to bring their wives with them to Mongolia or to marry Mongol women. More important than the law was Chinese custom. The Chinese who went to distant, un-Chinese regions like Mongolia, Sinkiang, or Tibet did not take his wife with him. If he had one, he left her in his father's household, where she often had a grim time of it, as a sort of unpaid servant. When he got to Mongolia, this Chinese "took on" a Mongol girl,

* There were exceptions to this in parts of Inner Mongolia where the Mongols had become more agricultural than pastoral. Here Mongols and Chinese peasants occasionally combined.

if his income permitted it. The idea was that if he made enough money, he would eventually return to China, and abandon the Mongol girl and her children. But Mongol women make loving and diligent wives and mothers, and such men often became very much attached to their "temporary" households. Moreover, in these years of stress most of these men heard no news from home except news of war lords, political uncertainty, and economic hardship.

It is also true, and important, that the higher the station in life of a Chinese, the more likely he was to be arrogant toward the Mongols and to consider them dirty, lazy, ignorant, barbarous. Humbler Chinese, on the other hand, normally came not only to like the Mongols but to admire them as honest, simple, straightforward, and trustworthy—the kind of people who would not betray friendship for money; while the Chinese society had been penetrated and corrupted enough by money values to set the dollar, all too often, above the man.

For these reasons there was an outcome surprising to those who accept the old clichés about the Chinese absorbing everyone with whom they come in contact, without themselves being changed. In Mongolia, with each wave of crisis, wealthy Chinese went back to China, but poor Chinese—usually those who were happy with a Mongol wife and family—stayed on. The children grew up speaking the mother's language better than the father's. They have not been discriminated against, and are now accepted as completely Mongol. They are to be found in Ulan Bator, especially in the chains of small stores, co-operatively organized, that sell food and consumer goods.

What is important politically is that in the revolutionary period these Chinese had no significant ideological influence on the Mongols. They were not themselves revolutionary, being cut off from new ideas going around in their own country. On the contrary, it was the Mongols who influenced the Chinese. When a Chinese decided to stay in Mongolia he was saying to himself, in fact, that everything was collapsing back home, that it was bad in Mongolia too, but that he had learned to trust the Mongols and had decided to stick with them.

Contact with the Russians was as different as it could be. A great part of the frontier with Siberia was open country, easily crossed. The forward zone of Cossack and peasant colonization was not one of close settlement. The Chinese colonizing farmer always took up land beside another colonist, creating a patch of "the Chinese way of life" that excluded everything else. The Siberian Russian, given an axe, a gun, and a plough, often liked to sally out far ahead of the general line of advance. Forests with open meadows were one of his favorite landscapes. Here he could plough a little, hunt a little, keep a few horses and cows, and a few hives of bees. Unlike the Chinese, he was a milk drinker and so kept cows as well as oxen. The Chinese confronted the Mongols with an alternative, almost an ultimatum: either herding or farming, but not both. Russian contact suggested to the Mongols diversification, without completely letting go of their old ways.

Politically also the contacts were quite different. In 1911 the Chinese and the Mongols had revolted against an alien dynasty, that of the Manchus, and this gave a chauvinistic slant to both Chinese and Mongol nationalism. In 1905 the Russians had revolted against their own

Tsar, not a foreigner, and had lighted a fuse that was to set off greater explosions in 1917 and 1918. The Russian Empire, moreover, was differently constructed from any other empire. Western empires were created by small numbers of people who crossed wide seas and oceans and imposed themselves as small elites. A caste-like color antagonism was added to class antagonism: "we whites are ruling races, you colored peoples are subject races." But the Tsarist Empire had expanded on vast, continuous land fronts. The soldiers and the administrators were followed by peasants, artisans, and manual laborers. As in no other empire, the poor and the illiterate of the conquered peoples had a good deal of contact with those of their conquerors who were not really conquerors but, like themselves, poor, illiterate, and without political rights. Class, in the long pull, was inevitably more important than color. Sometimes ordinary Russians did behave barbarously toward ordinary "natives"; but in major crises, including "native rebellions," those of the conquered peoples who had property to safeguard, and many of whom had become associated with the lower and even the middle ranks of the Tsarist structure of authority, tended to side with "law and order," while of those Russians who were "subjects" rather than "citizens" many fraternized with the conquered peoples.

These tendencies were sharpened by the activities of the many Russian, Ukrainian, and Polish political exiles in Siberia. No other empire helped to dig its own grave as the Tsarist Empire did by concentrating its own political dissidents in its own colonial fringe. These exiles did a great deal of the pioneer work in the scientific study of the languages, societies, and history of Siberia, Central Asia, and Mongolia; and while they learned, many of them also taught, spreading political ideas and encouraging political organization.

In this way a number of currents converged in the revolutionary crisis of 1917 and 1918. The Mongols immediately had a demonstration, right in their own country, of what was going on in Russia. The Tsarist establishment included consular representation at Urga, Uliassutai, and Kobdo, each with an armed guard. Around these officials were grouped little Russian communities—various advisers to the Mongolian authorities, the headquarters of large trading concerns, a few shopkeepers, and a school in Urga which gave preliminary training to Mongols who were later sent on to schools in Siberia, in order to become interpreters and bureaucrats.

These communities were split by the revolutionary news. The higher officials and military officers assured the Mongols that Tsarism would be restored, and in the meantime demanded support and assistance. Down through the ranks, however, there were also sympathizers with all the factions that existed in Russia. There were even a number of Communists, who seem not to have been sent in by the Party to get things going in Mongolia, but were men who had quietly found jobs in Mongolia in order to escape surveillance in Siberia. Some were making their living as merchants on a small scale. Others were working, or had worked, for the Siberian co-operatives. Still others had jobs in or connected with the Tsarist Consulate, the printing press, and so on. There were many other radicals who, without being Bolsheviks, were bitterly opposed to the Tsarist regime. All were waiting for what we would now call the "moment of truth"—the coming of the Red Army—and all who spoke Mongol, or had Russian-speaking Mongol

friends, were quietly telling the Mongols to get ready
for a new dawn, the beginning of an entirely new day.

These splits among the Russians put pressure on the
Mongols who were in contact with them to think politically. There was, of course, the crude bandwagon choice
—if you thought one side was going to win, no matter
what you did yourself, then it was best to get on the
bandwagon of that side. But there were also more
sophisticated choices. If a man thought he knew what
Mongolia's national interest was, then which Russians
ought he to favor in order to promote that national interest? Since very few men are able to make a really dis-
passionate distinction between their idea of the national
interest and their instinctive concern for their own
interest, the mere contemplation of choice was likely to
divide Mongols on conservative and radical lines. Finally,
even Mongols who did not know much about politics
knew that they were not simply bystanders, watching
what was going on in Russia, because what was happening in Russia was happening in the context of renewed
pressure from China—known to every Mongol—and renewed Japanese activity on the eastern frontier.

The civil war in Siberia swayed back and forth, as
Allied intervention delayed Bolshevik victory. There was
time for defeated anti-Bolshevik detachments to straggle
across the frontier, hoping either to regroup and go back
to the war or to escape on across Mongolia into Manchuria; for Bolsheviks and other revolutionaries to slip
into Mongolia, hoping to hide out until the Red Army
got nearer; and later for Partisan bands to appear, skir-
mishing in advance of the main Red forces. The situation was made worse by marauding Chinese bands, and
the civilian population suffered terribly.

Material in Mongolia's National Archives shows that there were three main responses to the intensifying crisis. The highest government authorities were the most alarmed about the Communist danger. They assured the Tsarist consular representatives that they would support them and would not permit Soviet representatives, sent to replace them, to enter the country. They kept exhorting the frontier watchposts and patrols to tighten up their security and not to allow any infiltration by Communists, who were referred to as the "new party," or the "disorderly party." But the reaction of the people was different. The frontier officers kept reporting back that the situation was getting out of control, because everywhere the Reds appeared the people helped them, providing them with remounts and guides.

Finally, there was a response at an intermediate level, which I think may have been decisive. The territories of hereditary princes were called Banners. The Banners near the frontier were required to maintain regional levies, to back up the frontier patrols in just this kind of emergency. But a number of the princes realized that it was the anti-Bolshevik bands and the Chinese marauders who were doing the killing and plundering, and that unless they did something to protect their people they would lose whatever authority they had. So they began to use their light, poorly armed troops—mostly cavalry— as skirmishers, hanging on the flanks of the marauders, killing stragglers, and once in a while ambushing a whole detachment; and as soon as the new Partisan bands appeared, they not only supported them but, in a few instances, merged their troops with them.

What had come about, in fact, was a classical revolutionary conjuncture. Only a few revolutionaries were following a plan of action, but they were able to draw in a large following of people desperate for leadership and in a mood to follow the leadership that seemed most resolute. Between themselves and this mass following they were able to fit in a coalition of groups who agreed with them on this or that immediate aim, but whose ultimate aim was only to reform the old national order, not to substitute for it a new revolutionary order. A conjuncture of this kind does not always result in the success of the revolution; but when it does, it simultaneously prepares the ground for a post-revolutionary crisis of adjustment between what has been achieved and what some think still remains to be done.

This crisis of adjustment was reached in Mongolia in 1921 when the Soviet Union, after defeating counter-revolution and Allied intervention in Siberia, became strong enough to send Red Army detachments into Mongolia. Red Russians, revolutionary Mongols, and nationalist Mongols together defeated the Chinese remnants and Ungern-Sternberg, and marched on Urga.

5

A Revolution of Shepherds

IN 1961, to celebrate the fortieth anniversary of the Mongolian People's Republic, the Mongols published an extraordinary book. It contains the personal stories of 203 men who in 1921 joined the Partisans of Suke-bator, the fiery young cavalryman and machine-gunner turned revolutionary. Those who could write, wrote their own. The stories of others were taken down by dictation or by tape-recorder. They were not dressed up by literary editing, but are as the men told them. They give sometimes almost blinding glimpses of what revolution is. But after forty years men's memories get hazy here and there, and sometimes two eyewitnesses do not agree. These discrepancies were not smoothed out. I commented to several Mongols that I admired this presentation very much: it was history in the raw. Their answers were in almost the same words: "But how else would you do it? Later on, the historians can straighten things out. But in the meantime, these men were there. These are their stories, and they have a right to tell them."

In these 203 stories the outside world is given, for the first time, some notion of what the men were like who fought for revolution in Mongolia—what parts of the country they came from, their social classification, their age-groups, what they had been doing before they decided to join up and fight. What they did after the revolution is sometimes mentioned, sometimes not.

Rough figures drawn from these personal stories show a vivid cross section of Mongol society at that time, and many evidences of its disarray. About one-third of the men had served in the national army, regional levies, the military police, or the guards posted along the Siberian frontier. Several had even been in the bodyguard of the Urga Living Buddha. A dozen had been lama priests or monks—mostly when they were young. Another dozen had been orphans, or had been given away for adoption by parents too poor to bring them up. More than a dozen had been farmers or part-time farmers. A sort of lower intelligentsia element, in an age of prevalent illiteracy, is indicated by nine men who had been scribes in the civilian or military bureaucracies. One who had attended a Chinese school in Urga, and then been a telegrapher, had also "taught Mongol, Manchu, Chinese, Russian, and English." He was less than 30 years old when he joined in organizing the first party congress of the new Revolutionary Party.

One man was from the small Mongol minority in Uryankhai—later the People's Republic of Tannu-Tuva and still later annexed by Russia; one was a Buryat from Siberia. Five were Mongols from Sinkiang, followers of a nationalist noble who, preferring a Tsarist Russian sphere of influence to life in a Chinese-ruled province, had in 1911 moved from Sinkiang through Russian territory into eastern Mongolia. One was a Chinese. As a boy, a waif, he had wandered into Mongolia. There were quite a few Chinese of this kind in the old Mongolia.

By far the largest of the overlapping categories that can be set up out of the data in these personal stories is that of men who had worked here and there as hired herdsmen, hunters, caravan men, cart-drivers in the old official transportation service, and stage-riders in the courier service. To be a stage-rider was a tough and much hated life. Nominally, all commoners could be conscripted to ride the stages, carrying official orders or escorting official travelers, but anyone who had any money at all paid a substitute to ride for him, and so only the poorest men took on the job. This category can be widened or narrowed by including in it, or setting apart in a different category, those who had also had a few cattle of their own, but not enough to make their families economically independent.

About half of the Partisans were men from eastern Mongolia and about one-third from the west, leaving some 15 per cent of scattered and sometimes unknown origin. These proportions are about what one would expect. Eastern Mongolia was more revolutionary than the west. The westerners were very militant, but up to this point they had been politically more nationalist than revolutionary. There had in fact always been differences, and certain kinds of antagonism, between eastern and western Mongolia. Chingis Khan had been a man of the east, and in order to unite Mongolia he had had to conquer the tribes of the west. In recent centuries the Jebtsundamba Hutukhtu or "Living Buddha of Urga," the holiest figure in the Mongolian Lama Buddhist hierarchy, who since 1911 had also been the head of the state, taking the title of Khagan, had been identified with the ascendancy of the east over the west. Crossed by the great trade route from Kalgan in China to Kyakhta in Siberia, and penetrated as well by Chinese trade from the Manchurian provinces in the east, with Urga as both the capital of religious conservatism and the point of maximum concentration of alien and modern influences, eastern Mongolia had a structure of authority externally more feudal, and an economy and society internally more eroded, than the west. It was full of men who had drifted away from the old Mongol life. It was the obvious region in which to look for both discontent and repression, and for the tinder awaiting the revolutionary spark: and in fact both Sukebator and Choibalsang, the men who struck the spark, were men of the east.

Western Mongolia had been conquered by the Manchus later than the east. Although its institutions of authority were much less impressive than those of the east, it was proud of being the stronghold of "the old Mongol ways." Like the east, it had been impoverished by debts to Chinese traders and money-lenders, but in spite of poverty its structure had been less disrupted than that of the east. It was much farther from the railways of both Siberia and China, and its trade routes to Siberia were more mountainous, and those to China ran across much greater distances of desert. Like the east, it had its own great princes and Living Buddhas. They were very conservative, and completely loyal to the Living Buddha of Urga, but at the same time they tenaciously defended the regional autonomy of the west and their own rights and privileges against encroachment by the underlings of the Urga Living Buddha.

The west, to sum it all up, was the part of Mongolia

in which to look for an intense Mongol nationalism and a quasi-racial dislike of the Chinese within a horizon limited, in the years of crisis, by the idea that, if only all foreign intruders could be thrown out, the good old days would come back. These had in fact been the characteristics western Mongolia had shown in 1911, when the Manchu Empire fell. In the west, Manchu garrisons and Chinese traders had been massacred, while in the east they had been allowed to escape; in the west, there had been continuing resistance to Chinese debt and damage claims, while at Urga, the national capital, interested parties had never ceased to urge "accommodations."

The data, however, also bring out some of the complexities of life and politics. Among the eastern rank and file of the Partisans, only a very few were personal followers of Sukebator and Choibalsang from the beginning. Speaking in a general way, most of them were men who joined an organized revolutionary movement as soon as there was one to join. The men of the west, on the other hand, though fewer in number—one-third as against one-half—had practically all of them rallied to the leadership of a single man, a leader famous as the "Warrior of the West" long before the names of Sukebator and Choibalsang were known. Had it not been for his own choice, he could have made for himself a military "cult of personality" clashing with the loyalty to an organization of the easterners. The choice he made is one of the keys to an understanding of the Mongol Revolution.

The man in question was Maksarjab, a strange, romantic, and sometimes savage figure. Had events run a little differently, he might easily have been a "Cossack" kind of nationalist leader, intense but narrow, one of the first to fight against aliens but later leading a last-stand resistance to social revolution among his own people.* He was of the lesser nobility, a descendant not of Chingis Khan but of a commoner who had been ennobled by the Manchus for valor in fighting against Moslem insurgents in Sinkiang in the nineteenth century. He had been poor as a boy and had lived by farming, as did a good many Mongols in his part of the west. He had made himself famous in the fighting against Manchus and Chinese in 1911, and later, commanding troops on every frontier of Mongolia except that with Siberia, he had repelled both Chinese war-lord attacks and the attempts of Inner Mongolian leaders to impose a "Pan-Mongol" leadership on Outer Mongolia.

He was imprisoned by the Chinese under "Little" Hsü and later joined up for a while with Baron Ungern-Sternberg, because the "Mad Baron" was dislodging the last Chinese war-lord invaders from Urga. He also served briefly as Minister of War in the puppet government that Ungern-Sternberg set up under the Urga Living Buddha. Then came the turning point. Because this government was the puppet of a foreign adventurer, he went over to the movement led by his juniors, Sukebator and Choibalsang, which he thought truly national—thus abandoning personal ambition at a moment when he could have put himself at the head of a blindly devoted following of soldiers. He died in the middle 1920's.

The Partisans who described this period picture a society in which for most of the common people, and

* There is a biography of him, in Mongol, written by Choibalsang, which as far as I know has never been translated. See Owen Lattimore, *Nationalism and Revolution in Mongolia*, p. 64 and footnote.

even for some of the less fortunately placed aristocracy
and clergy, poverty was always there or just around the
corner, and many families were unable to hold together.
At the same time, there was a large supply of men who
could ride a horse, handle a gun, or engage successfully
in one of a number of occupations. This is quite different from a conventional picture of Asia, with its land-
bound peasantry of circumscribed activity, and it helps
to explain why the Mongols have never thought of themselves as especially "Asian," or been susceptible to Pan-
Asian propaganda; indeed the Mongols are more akin
to the Siberian Cossacks and peasants, with their exten-
sive agriculture and relatively large number of livestock, than to the intensive, "garden"-farming Chinese,
with their almost total lack of livestock.

The picture is also much more "revolutionary" than
that to be found in the travel books of, say, the period
from 1870 to 1910, which describe a poor but meek,
ignorant, and helpless people—with a few exceptions like
Pozdneev, who knew the language well and had glimpses
of the dark wrath under the surface. There are para-
doxes even along the advanced skirmish-line of revolution, however. Of the 203 surviving Partisans who here
tell their stories, only eight are listed as already Party
members in 1921; another four joined in 1922. Five
more joined later—one as late as 1940: a total of only
seventeen out of all these combat heroes of the critical
year 1921. The significance of this low figure is confirmed by the fact that very few of this picked group
rose to really high position in later life. I was told that
longer biographies of a number of leaders are to be
published separately, and of course the lives of the three
greatest—Sukebator, Choibalsang, and Maksarjab—are

already well known to all Mongols; but, still, these
stories of the rank and file are enough to show that the
Mongol Revolution had from the beginning the marks of
Communist organizing principle: it had a hard core of
"professional" revolutionaries, who did not recruit even
brave and patriotic soldiers into their Party ranks unless
they had also exactly the right political personalities.

In this context it is easy to understand the careers and
personalities of Sukebator and Choibalsang, the two
front-line heroes of Mongolia's 1921 Revolution. Both
were men of the people, but both led lives which, while
not removing them from contact with what ordinary
people thought and felt, gave them experiences and contacts ramifying far beyond those of ordinary people. Both
were literate in their own language, which most ordinary
Mongols were not, and both knew a foreign language,
Russian—Sukebator having, it seems, a fair knowledge
and Choibalsang a good one. Before the opening of the
revolutionary chapter Sukebator had been trained by
Russian professional soldiers, had fought well, and was
widely known and admired by the ordinary soldier;
Choibalsang had lived among radical Russian students
in Siberia.

Sukebator was born in a very poor family, in 1893.
His father was an "internal displaced person"—a man
who had left his own "Banner" or tribal territory to
wander about looking for work. He succeeded so poorly
that he had to give away a daughter for adoption. At the
age of fourteen Sukebator rode the post-stages or courier-
stages—a hated duty, as I have mentioned above. In spite
of all this, he also managed to pick up an education, at
least to the extent of writing his own language. How

this could happen needs perhaps a word of explanation
for the Western reader.

In a feudal society, with its balance of privileges and
duties, both determined by birth, the son of a "good"
family, if he could read and write, might be summoned
for several years of boring duty in the bureacracy of the
state. There were no regular schools. The sons of the
well-to-do studied either in the family or under a tutor.
It was a good idea for a tutor to take on, now and then,
a clever boy from a very poor family. Then he would be
able to do a good turn for a well-off family, if it had
a son summoned for service, by providing an acceptable
substitute. A tutor also often had more affection for a
non-paying disciple than for paying students. Sukebator's
tutor later became a trusted political confidant. (Another
way of evading service was to educate a son in reading
only, but not writing; then, if he were examined, he
would write such a hopelessly poor hand that he would
be excused.)

In 1912, just after the 1911 Revolution, Sukebator was
conscripted into the new national army at the age of
nineteen and served in a "new style" unit trained by
Russian officers. The history of these forces shows one
aspect of the bankruptcy of leadership in the Mongol
ruling classes. Although the nobles had a military tradition, they would not go into the ranks of such units in
order to get a grounding in modern warfare. They did
not even bother to fill the ranks with trusted followers
who still had something of the old feudal loyalty. Conscripted out-of-works, like Sukebator, were considered
good enough. The result was that an elite developed in
the ranks and among the under-officers, promoted from

the ranks: men who had mastered the weapons and the tactics, and whom the others followed out of personal devotion. Sukebator served for nine years, until his unit was demobilized in 1919 by the Chinese, after their return to Mongolia. He tried to hide arms instead of turning them in to the Chinese, to keep in touch with the men of his unit, and to keep them standing by for future action.

This was the origin of Sukebator's political career. Because it was known that he had support among the unwillingly disbanded troops, it was easy for him to make contact with others who wanted to resist a sell-out to the Chinese militarists. Although his official biography does not say so in so many words, it seems that Sukebator was not yet guided by Communist or any other theory. What he did have was political instinct, and his instinct was to work with everybody who was in favor of resistance—and this included many of the old regime, especially in the lower ranks—so that he would have contacts leading in as many directions as possible. He was, at the same time, a tough realist, who carefully sorted out his contacts until he knew who was useful chiefly for communication with people outside the group, who was in the group but would waver under pressure, and whom he could count on as the hard core of resistance, ready for anything. The influence of political theory came later, through Sukebator's contact with Choibalsang, and Choibalsang's already close contact with Russian Communists.

Choibalsang also came from a poor family, in the plains of eastern Mongolia where he was born in 1895. At the age of thirteen he was put in a monastery by his pious mother, but at the age of seventeen he ran away—

not at all an uncommon thing to do—and began to lead a wandering, casual, odd-job life. He made for Urga, the center of excitement as the capital of the new Autonomous Mongolia. Although autonomy, with Tsarist Russian support, obviously meant the possibility of many new occupations, it was a weakness of the upper classes in civilian as in military life that they did not want to go into any new occupation except at the top. Let the poor people fill the bottom ranks. This provided an opening for Choibalsang to be recruited into a school for interpreters. He then went on to a higher school at Irkutsk, in Siberia. There, with his Russian fellow-students, he heard of the Russian Revolution. The Mongol students were then called home, to keep them away from the revolutionary infection. (The Mongol sources say no more than this—perhaps because the really significant Russian influence on Choibalsang was after his return to Mongolia.)

A regime that is about to collapse seems to go into a partial paralysis, a strange combination of strong negative action and inability to act positively. The old regime in Mongolia was unable to recruit from its own ranks a young intelligentsia that it could trust, but it was not too dull-witted to realize that the young intellectuals and the young soldiers who were beginning to multiply in those ranks of society that did not belong to "the best people" did not have the interests of "the best people" at heart. Since those whom it could trust were useless in dealing with the new problems that were crowding in, while those who understood the new problems knew that they could only be dealt with if very great changes were forced on the old regime, the internal crisis took the form of a struggle by the old regime to smother everything that looked like a new initiative, a new move. This made reform impossible and revolution inevitable, by forcing the activists to look outside for revolutionary aid.

In this phase Sukebator represented the fire and zeal of revolutionary nationalism, while Choibalsang was the pioneer in setting up organizational connections between revolution in Mongolia and international revolution. Sukebator and Choibalsang were at first unknown to each other. Sukebator organized a resistance group after the Chinese demobilized his military unit. Choibalsang organized a separate group after he was recalled from school in Siberia. The difference between these groups was that Sukebator was in touch with many nationalists who were not really revolutionaries. Some of them were functionaries of the civil and ecclesiastical establishments whose ideas did not go much beyond getting the Chinese out and getting Mongols back into the controlling positions. From the very beginning Choibalsang was in touch with Russian Communists. From them he took over the idea that a world revolution had already broken out in which the Russians, much more numerous and powerful than the Mongols, were taking the lead, but the Mongols, if they followed the Russians, would have nothing to fear. This was to be a new kind of revolution. Going far beyond the rebellion of an oppressed nation against imperialist rule, it would make it possible for the downtrodden and disinherited within each nation to join with those in other nations.

The force of this appeal can be judged both by the roll-call of those who responded to it and the roster of those who fought against it to the last. Fragmentary though it is, the material on the Mongol Partisans shows the wide possibilities of recruitment among men who no longer felt that they belonged in the old structure of prince and tribe, "Banner" and region, or social unit co-ordinated with economic and political functions. In these structures they found no shelter from the events that were raging about them; why should they support a system that gave them nothing in return? At the same time the contrast was always before their eyes: at the last moment of crisis a handful of priests and princes of the old establishment had always compromised with a "Little" Hsü, an Ungern-Sternberg—foreigners backed by foreign powers, the Japanese operating from Manchuria, the Allied intervention in Siberia.

The setting favored a fusion of militant nationalism and revolutionary internationalism. From the way the Partisans tell their stories it is clear that they were responding to an appeal to rid the country of the freebooting gangs of Chinese militarists and Tsarist Russians. In Siberia, the resistance leaders had the same battle cry, rallying everybody, Russians and Buryats, to clear out the foreign intervention. But the Partisans also represented the Mongols who had lost faith in the traditional leaders—the men who had always made deals with foreigners, and were now associating with their counterparts, the Russian leaders who did not stick at using foreign troops and foreign money to try to force their own people into submission. The Mongol Partisan was a man whose response was to make common cause with the Siberian Partisans and the regular Red Army.

It must also be remembered that this was the "romantic" phase of revolution in Siberia. Against the horrors of civil war and the brutalities of foreign military intervention rose the banner of internationalism. The Russian revolutionaries in Siberia had been joined by a sprinkling of released prisoners of war—Germans, Austrians, German and Austrian Poles, and all the nationalities of the Austro-Hungarian Empire. The man who organized the Far Eastern Republic, which served briefly as a buffer between the Soviet Union and the Allied intervention, was a Russian—not a Siberian—who as a radical student had escaped to America; when it came to drafting a constitution for a republic, he had to do it in English.

The stream of revolution in Mongolia began to flow into this larger torrent after Sukebator and Choibalsang, each organizing his own underground resistance group, had come into contact with each other. They instantly hit it off, and no jealousy seems ever to have marred their friendship. Sukebator, Mongol nationalist and man of action, was impatient because action was denied him by the dangerously strong Ungern-Sternberg forces and the Chinese war-lord remnants which, though demoralized, were still much better armed then the Mongols. For him, linking up with the Soviet revolution meant not simply an internationalizing of the Mongol movement, but, above all, and at last, a chance for the Mongols to go into action on their own soil and in their own cause, because the men and arms which could be expected from Siberia would give him just the extra margin which, as a professional soldier, he knew he had to have. For Choibalsang, whose underground organization was already part Russian, part Mongol, Sukebator was the ideal ally; he brought in a striking arm that was not only Mongol and national, but more widely national than narrowly revolutionary.

This decisive alliance, out of which grew the Mongolian People's Revolutionary Party, was formed in the winter of 1919-20. Early in 1920 an agent of the Comintern named I. Sorokovikov succeeded in getting through into Mongolia, and from then on his advice confirmed the new tendencies in the Mongolian revolutionary movement. His accounts of what went on in this period are still cited as authoritative by Mongol historians. It is to be remembered that in this phase of the Revolution, when the Bolsheviks thought that their movement had a good chance of quickly taking over the whole world, the delegates who were sent to Mongolia and other countries were accredited by the Comintern rather than by the Russian Communist Party.

No revolutionary history has been more neglected by the outside world than that of Mongolia. Now, after forty years of indifference, Mongolia has become a member of the United Nations. This combination makes for a sudden convergence of interest, from several directions, and for an easy assumption that Mongolia's history, in these decades, has been made entirely from the outside. The Mongols must, the argument goes, have been so few and weak, so lacking in knowledge of how to organize a nation and administer a state, that all the Soviet Union had to do, once the Red Army was strong enough to pursue its enemies (like Ungern-Sternberg) into Mongol territory, was to seize the main line of communications from the Siberian frontier to the capital, garrison the capital, appoint a few political agents of its own, and recruit a few Mongols willing to work for Russian overlords. "Little" Hsü had done this for a while, Ungern-Sternberg had done it for a while, and a Red Russian state would be able to do it as long as it liked, once the international intervention forces had been driven out of Siberia.

But history most nearly comes alive when there is enough in the records to go beyond a recital of the events and to recover, for the reader of today, something of how people felt while the events were happening. There is a great deal of this kind of material available in Mongolia; in the memories of people who lived through those times, and in extremely interesting written records. This material makes it quite clear that the Mongol view is that they themselves took the initiative. Sukebator and Choibalsang became political heroes, in addition to being military heroes, because they were convinced that Soviet Russia would help Mongolia if asked. On this conviction they risked their lives to get through the lines and make contact with the Russian revolutionaries. They got through; they got the help; and they came back with it.

Thus the Mongol way of putting it is the exact opposite of saying: "The Russians intervened, with the result that we became obligated to them and have remained obligated ever since." What the Mongols say is: "The Russians came in with the kind of help we had asked for. They stayed while we set up a new government. It was a compromise government, and it remained a compromise government for several years, because we did not want liberation from our foreign enemies to be followed by civil war among ourselves. When the military situation was stabilized, they withdrew their troops; but they remained our allies, which was lucky for us, because the danger from Chinese militarists and Japanese imperialists receded for a few years, but was far from over. Of course we had to go on asking for aid, and we were lucky to have allies who gave it to us without taking over control, or forcing us to join the Soviet Union."

If this version looks too much like the bright colors of a "socialist brotherhood" propaganda poster, it can be toned down. There are drab colors, too, on the palette of Mongolian history. The problem of the historian is that of the painter summoned to paint the portrait of Oliver Cromwell—"not to leave out the warts," but in painting in the warts, not to deface the greatness of the subject.

6

The Real Revolution Begins

IN THE HISTORY of revolutions, it is only after the Revolution has triumphed that the real revolution begins. This proposition is not hard to understand. For Americans, it is classically stated in Charles A. Beard's theory of the American Revolution—that when it began about one-third of the people of the thirteen colonies were in favor of it, about one-third were loyal to the British monarchy, and about one-third undecided, and that it took the British seven years to make enough mistakes to force the undecided third over to the side of the revolutionary third. The typical revolution is in fact not so much won by the winners as lost by the losers. The winners are a coalition, and only in part a coalition of groups which have freely joined with each other to carry out a common purpose; in large part the members of the coalition have been forced to travel in company with each other by a government which they would have liked to reform, not to overthrow, but which by its blundering misuse of its own waning power has left them no choice but rebellion.

Under such conditions the partly convergent, partly divergent aims of those who have joined the coalition cannot be clarified in the course of the struggle to overthrow the old order. It is in this sense that the "real" revolution begins only after the overthrow, because a new order must now be installed. Since the specifications for it could not be agreed in advance, the alternatives between building a new order according to one theory or some other theory involve different distributions of power. This is the "real" revolution, because there is no room for forgiveness of mistakes, no time for compromising adjustments between theory and practice. There is a naked confrontation between aspiration, or theory, and reality, or power, and the slightest miscalculation in theory must be paid for on the spot in loss of power—and the power which is "lost" is not in fact lost, but passes into other hands.

Nevertheless, the victorious Mongol revolutionaries walked very cautiously in their first years of power. Their most striking concession to conservative nationalism was to leave the Living Buddha in his position as Head of State, though stripping him of his autocratic executive powers, which were transferred to a Cabinet of Ministers; the ministries, in turn, were controlled, though as yet by no means fully staffed, by revolutionaries. In this way deference to a symbol of continuity was combined with a decisive shift in the distribution of real power. The balance of compromise thus established lasted until the death of the Living Buddha in 1924.

If, in those days of the early 1920's, you were a Russian revolutionary, you were likely to see Mongolia as an important but still subordinate factor in the larger problems of Japan and China. The Soviet Union had

recovered all of Siberia. Japanese imperialism was in
retreat: but Russia's main concern now must be the
economic revival of ravaged Siberia, not a policy of
expansion that would make the Western nations approve
of Japanese countermeasures. In any case it was clearly
in China, not in Mongolia, that new events were shaping
up. In North China, the war-lord government in Peking
was hostile and suspicious; but still a Soviet envoy,
A. A. Joffe, had been received in Peking in 1922 (followed by L. Karakhan in 1923), and negotiations were
possible. The Soviet Union should not make them more
difficult by trying to force China to recognize the independence of Mongolia. In South China, a Communist
Party had been founded, the Soviet Union had made
a friendly contact with Sun Yat-sen, and co-operation
between Chinese Communists and Nationalists was beginning. Here lay the hope for really revolutionary developments, and the Mongolian question should be left
in abeyance, because the more revolutionary the outcome in China, the greater the likelihood of a friendly
settlement between revolutionary Chinese and revolutionary Mongols.

As for Mongolia itself, there was nothing to worry
about. It was clear that men like Sukebator and Choibalsang trusted the Soviet Union, and therefore the Russians could trust them. The thing to do was to help the
revolutionaries to get their government and their economy going, but, because of poor communications and
total lack of industry, a drastic program was not possible. The powers of the nobility and the clergy should
be whittled down enough to enable the revolutionaries
to keep the upper hand, but there was no need to push
class hostility too far, precipitating civil war. In view of

the lack of a Mongol middle class of merchants and entrepreneurs, the most promising line of development would be to promote consumer co-operatives and foreign trade co-operatives.

If in those years you were a conservative Mongol, you were likely to feel that you had had a narrow escape, but that the outlook for the future was quite hopeful. At least the country was now independent. True, there were Russian troops garrisoned in Mongolian territory; but the Russians were not trying to take over the government of the country, and that being the case there was a definite advantage in the presence of Russian troops. It meant that the Chinese could not return, gun in hand; and as long as the Chinese could not dictate terms, a conservative Mongol with money and social prestige could get along comfortably and profitably with individual Chinese traders. Of course there were some new laws on the books, canceling debts and abolishing the hereditary right to collect certain kinds of tribute; but a man of family and substance still had social prestige. The people had been stirred up, but they had not lost all their respect for the nobility and for men who had held office and could read documents. They would still listen to you when you told them what to do about their problems.

Suppose, for example, a certain Chinese firm had always dominated the trade in your district. It could no longer collect the debts owed to it, which had been canceled by law, but with the return of peace its representative was coming around again, trying to work up some new trade. You could say to the man, "I think this debt cancellation business is a shame. After all, an honest trader deserves his profit; there's nothing wrong about

that. If you and I went into partnership, I could get
your money back for you. I could explain to the people
that you can offer better credit than these new co-operatives; but if you give credit, the people should start
paying you installments on what they owe from the
past. And besides that, what about going in together on
one of those motor trucks? That seems to be the latest
thing. One truck can carry as much as ten or twenty
camels, and do the trip much faster. You get hold of a
good American truck down in China and drive it up
here, and I'll see that you get the trade."

If in those years you had been a Mongol revolutionary
your views would largely have been framed for you,
I think, on the one hand by the cautious policy of Soviet
Russia and on the other hand by the still great strength
of the nobility and the clergy. The revolutionaries had
won a victory, but not a victory giving them complete
freedom of action. They were popular heroes—to have
fought in the Partisan ranks was to belong to a new elite
—but the popularity won on the battlefield could easily
be eroded by mistakes in the less glamorous business of
government and administration. They had in their own
ranks very few men with experience in economic organization or ordinary bureaucratic paper-shuffling. The
literacy rate was very low, and they could not train their
own men in a hurry. For some years they would have to
rely, in the ordinary routine of running a country, on
men whose outlook was more conservatively nationalistic than revolutionary, and of these many would not
really believe in, and some would actively sabotage, the
policies they were asked to carry out.

With these limitations in mind, it is not hard to understand what the revolutionaries did, and why they did

what they did. They had two sets of priorities: measures to strengthen their own party, and measures to weaken, forestall, and split the actual and potential opposition.

The party that rules Mongolia has from the beginning called itself the Mongolian People's Revolutionary Party. Mongols will tell you today, "We're Marxist-Leninists—it's just the same as having a Communist Party"—but, historically, the absence of the word "Communist" is significant. In November 1921 a Mongol delegation which included Sukebator visited Moscow and conferred with Lenin. The Mongols, delighted with the success of their Russian alliance and wanting to show themselves diligent students in the Russian school of revolution, asked Lenin if they should not change the name of their party and call themselves Communists. Lenin advised against it. The Mongols, he said, had a pastoral nomadic society; it would not be appropriate to try to deal with its problems through a party of proletarian type. He urged them to develop toward socialism along a line by-passing the capitalist stage of economic and social history. This could be done largely through the promotion of co-operatives. In other words—if they would get down to the job of changing their society, they would find that out of this changing society recruits of a new kind would be entering their party ranks, and thus in time the party would be changed from within. The Mongols are very proud of having received and acted on this personal advice, directed squarely at their own problems; they consider that it gives them a special place in the history of revolutionary parties, and indeed it does distinguish their course of development from that of, for example, the Chinese Communists.

But there were also immediate problems. The People's

Revolutionary Party was not "monolithic" like that of
the Bolsheviks; it was in part a coalition. In 1921, when
they had set up their first government, the revolutionaries installed as Premier and commander in chief of
the army a man named Bodo. He had been one of the
original twenty members of Sukebator's underground
group. He was a former lama who had been a disciple
of the Living Buddha and had had important administrative experience. For these reasons he was probably
very useful to the underground group in the days when
it needed to be able to make contacts in various directions; but after coming to power he was accused of
having leagued himself with Chinese merchants, some
of whom in turn had foreign backing, and with members
of the Living Buddha's former government, in a plot to
restore theocratic monarchy. He was shot.

In the context of the time, and remembering that
revolutionaries who have just come to power are patho-
logically afraid of counter-attacks by those whom they
have just displaced, it is not surprising that he was con-
victed of treason. In analyzing a tragedy of this kind—
for even in treason there is tragedy—one part of the
historian's duty is to try to see through Mongol eyes.
If he fails in this, the atmosphere and mood of time and
place—right or wrong—cannot be brought before the
reader. But if he is not a Mongol, another part of his
duty is to go over what happened with the detachment
of a foreigner. I am not sure about the particular case
of Bodo, but my feeling in some cases is that men were
accused of treason when in fact they were not nerving
themselves to great ethical decisions between "treason"
and "loyalty," but merely making day-to-day, short-
range, humanly selfish moves in what they thought was

their own interest. "My rival is getting A and B lined up on his side. How can I protect my position? Whom can I get hold of? And what do I have to give him or promise him?" The Mongols—and they deserve great credit for it—have been going over the records and clearing the reputations of men they now think were unjustly condemned. Rehabilitation does not bring the dead back to life, but it is better than saying, cynically, "The man's dead—so who cares? Why drag up all that old stuff?"

On the other scale of priorities, that of dealing with the opposition, the revolutionaries did rather well. They correctly judged that the nobles were more hated than the religious hierarchy, and therefore attacked the nobles first, isolated the church and left it to be dealt with later. The nobles represented inheritance, and therefore divided inheritance, with more nobles, in each generation, trying to squeeze equally large incomes out of decreasing numbers of *khamjlaga* ("retainers"; frequently translated "serfs") and *albat* ("people who may be called on for tribute and service"). Within the structure of the feudal pyramid there were those who inherited office, with administrative, military, and juridical functions, and others—younger sons and branch lines—who inherited only titles of honor and a status that gave them a claim, legally imprecise but socially strong, to be "supported in the manner to which they were accustomed." Their claims were met by giving "dowry families" to the daughter of a great noble when she married, and "retainer families" to "sealless *taij*"—nobles claiming descent from Chingis Khan, but not inheriting a seal of office.

In this way, in spite of the general feudal principle that the main inheritance, especially the rule of territory, must pass in the senior line from father to son, there was a continuous parcellation of human resources. The "dowry" and "retainer" families had to support those to whom they were assigned, herding their cattle for them, making felt for their tents, providing domestic and labor service, accompanying them on journeys of state and on pilgrimages. Because of these duties they were supposed to be exempt from the general feudal services required of the *albat* families in each "banner" or tribal-feudal territory; but this only meant that every time there was a great wedding, or a distribution of retainers to younger sons after the death of a ruling prince, more families were assigned to the private service of privileged persons and fewer were left to carry the public burden of the "banner." Since the people who felt this increasingly cruel pressure could also see exactly how the machinery worked, the aristocracy was isolated as the main target of popular resentment.

In what Mongols call the "yellow" or religious feudal structure (because yellow is the sacred color of Tibetan Buddism), in the vast domains belonging to monasteries, the trend was in the opposite direction—toward accumulation instead of parcellation. Monasteries owned territory and had the right to administer and tax the secular population in such territory. Within the monastery, there was one structure for the regulation of religious life and another for economic management. The religious rule was authoritarian, and functions were delegated from the top. Economic ownership and management were in theory egalitarian. The property and income of a monastery, or of a "college" of Tibetan medicine or theology within a monastery, constituted its *jas*, a word meaning "collective property." In theory the *jas* belonged equally to all the monks of the "congregation," and they were supposed to elect managers from among themselves to supervise this property. In practice, the lamas who had religious authority and prestige had no difficulty in seeing that their own nominees were elected as managers and in drawing much more than equal shares from the common fund. In an example cited by a Mongol author, rank-and-file lamas were allocated three to five sheep a year for their own use—to eat or to sell—while highly placed lamas were drawing from twenty-five to one hundred sheep.

There were also lamas who were individually wealthy without holding high office. To give only one instance, a lama doctor, starting with animals presented to him by grateful or hopeful patients, could build up a big herd of livestock.

In addition there were, in round figures, a hundred Living Buddhas in the old Mongolia. Of these about a dozen were important enough to be on a special list requiring confirmation by the Manchu Emperor, but none was poor, some were wealthy, and the Living Buddha of Urga was fantastically wealthy. A Living Buddha's property, administered apart from but in conjunction with that of his monastery, was called his *sang* —from a Chinese word meaning "treasury." It included livestock and other kinds of property, it could include capital invested in a Chinese trading firm, but it did not include territory except in the case of the Urga Living Buddha, the Jebdsundamba Hutukhtu. It was possible for the pious to contribute to a Living Buddha's treasury in all kinds of ways. In one case a monastery created its fund or *jas* by levying a loan of animals on all the people of the region. At the end of three years these animals were returned, but the young animals born during the three years were retained, to constitute the monastery's "foundation" herd. A Living Buddha did not have to pay for herdsmen to look after his livestock. This was done for him by the *shabinar* of his monastery, as a feudal service. *Shabinar* (*shabi* in the singular), meaning "disciples," was the religious name given to the secular families who were the subjects of a monastic territory. A Living Buddha's treasury was a kind of trust fund, inherited after his death by the next "reincarnation."

Since most lamas were recruited by being placed in a monastery as children by their pious parents, there was a subsequent selective process within the ranks of the clergy. A few became mystics or ascetics, leading really holy lives. A few became scholars, and scholarship led to more diversity than might be expected in a stagnant society. Some were conservative and orthodox, others liberal and speculative. One reactionary leader—he was killed in the end by a special commando squad sent out to liquidate him—is quoted as having said that what Mongolia needed was not (as other conservatives maintained) more lamas, but "fewer and better lamas." There was even a monastery whose theological college speculated philosophically about the possibilities of reconciling the Buddhist, Christian, and Moslem religions.

Very few lamas, however, were intellectuals. Below the true intellectuals came the religious bureaucrats. The practitioners of Tibetan medicine were to be classified as adepts rather than as scientists—somewhat as in Western medicine, in which there are many superb technicians, but not so many real scientists. Below them again came monks who were artists and artisans—painters of religious pictures, metal workers casting bronze

images, carpenters and builders. The dull-witted or naturally submissive did menial and unskilled work.

In this grading of monkish activities one fact is conspicuous: generation after generation, the clergy was
able to recruit, within its own ranks, bureaucrats to
manage its domains, subjects, property, and tax and
trade revenues. Its affairs were more competently administered than those of most tribal or banner territories.
In addition, the church could protect its subjects from
military conscription and such *corvée* duties as riding
the courier-stages better than the princes could, and its
tax burdens were lower. Consequently church rule was
more popular than princely rule, and families tried to
escape, when they could, from princely territory to a
church domain. The system had bad consequences for
the nation, because it withdrew a large part of the manpower from the state, and perhaps as much as half of the
potential national revenue, and placed them under the
church's state within the state; but these were problems
that the new, socialistically oriented state could not even
get at until it had dealt with the "black" or secular feudalism. Once this had been done, the church was isolated
and the people were able to see more clearly its structure, the reckless expenditure of the revenues of a poor
country on ornate temples and costly images, the vulgar
display and "conspicuous consumption" of a few great
prelates, and the lines of cleavage between the men of
power in the church and the thousands and thousands
of ordinary lamas whose humble lives and activities were
not very different from those of the common people.

The first period of cautious adjustment, in which the
Revolutionary Party recruited wider popular support
chiefly by curtailing the feudal privileges of the nobility,

ended with the deaths of Sukebator in 1923 and the Living Buddha of Urga, fifteen months later, in 1924. The move against the nobility had been accompanied by a step toward inducting the people into self-government; both offices of local government and representation in the central government were thrown open to election. The step was not fully effective, however, because it was a reform brought about by pressure, not a seizure of power by revolutionary action. In the first years the nobles, who still held much of their wealth and prestige, were able to get either themselves or their own nominees elected to many positions supposedly representing the common people.

The most striking immediate result of the abolition of feudal rights was widespread internal migration. Thousands of people, previously forbidden to leave the jurisdiction of their princes, just packed up their tents, rounded up their herds, and went off wherever they wanted to go. The main shift of population was from the eastern into the western regions; I think this must have been because the Living Buddha's government had been strongest in the east, and people felt more autonomous in the west. Very likely also migration was a way of escaping from old debts—debts which had legally been cancelled, but which Chinese traders were still quietly and persistently trying to collect.

A little has been said already about Sukebator's origins and career. It should be added that he was a revolutionary cast in a purely Mongol mould. No leader of the new against the old could have been more different from the scholarly Lenin, Stalin the patient, power-hungry party organizer, or Sun Yat-sen who was essentially the liberal dreamer. Sukebator was a soldier and a gallant and romantic soldier, the young, handsome, generous "people's warrior." In 1922, at the *naadam* or summer games held to celebrate the first anniversary of the 1921 Revolution, Sukebator rode down the field at full gallop, leaning from the saddle to pick up silver dollars from the ground—a show to delight the cavalryman in every Mongol heart. Yet Sukebator was also of the poorest and most oppressed class, and as their champion he was not one who rose above them to rule them, but one who stepped out ahead to lead them. Since he had also the soldier's instinct for comradely loyalty, it was probably he even more than Choibalsang who from the beginning set the course of the Mongol revolution toward loyalty to the Russian alliance. He saw no derogation to Mongol dignity or pride in leading the Mongols as auxiliaries in a world revolution in which the Russians were the main body. He died young because his system had been weakened by tuberculosis; but officially the immediate cause of his death is declared to have been poison administered by a lama doctor.

While Sukebator's life was a short, heroic-tragic chapter ushering in a new Mongolia, that of the Jebdsundamba Hutukhtu was a long chapter in which were written all the details of the decay and squalid end of Mongolia's old order. He had pontificated for forty-nine years as the Mongolian primate of the Yellow Faith—as Mongols call Tibetan Buddhism—and for thirteen of these years he had also been the Head of State. Himself a Tibetan, he was the son of a sort of chamberlain of the Dalai Lama. He was a man of considerable ability, though dissolute.

In evaluating his career, it must be remembered that neither a Dalai Lama nor a Jebdsundamba Hutukhtu was a "pope" in the sense of having clearly defined insti-

tutional authority over lesser Living Buddhas, monasteries and their domains, or the qualifications, consecra-
tion, promotion, and discipline of the general clergy.
The great pontiffs reigned more than they ruled. They
could not rule by a precise, procedural, bureaucratic
code because distances were so great, communications so
poor, and literacy so scarce, that it was impossible to
command, from afar, the prompt information which such
a system requires.

In practice, the personal ascendancy of a Dalai or a
Jebdsundamba depended a great deal on whether he had
the kind of character that made lesser powers in the
church and the feudal structure turn to him of their
own accord for counsel and support. It was because the
last Urga Living Buddha did have this kind of character
that he stayed in the ascendancy for so long. Probably
this explains why Mongol (and Russian) writers are
rather surprisingly lenient in their accounts of him.
They could easily have made of him a sinister villain—
debauched, drunken, a lecher, a willful traitor, personally intent on destroying the revolution. Yet, instead of
describing him as a leading historical criminal, they
usually limit themselves to lumping him in with the
collective class enemies of the revolution, in such phrases
as "the feudal reactionaries, headed by the Living
Buddha." In some recent writing the personal attack on
him is stronger, but, even so, Mongol writers avoid
building up for him a "cult of personality" in reverse.

On the death of the Living Buddha in 1924 the first
symbolic test of strength was on the traditional procedure
of seeking, finding, and installing a "'reincarnation" or
successor—a procedure which included divination and
much maneuvering among factions within the church.

The revolutionaries announced that there were to be no more reincarnations of the Urga Living Buddha or any other "Incarnation," but this decision was still open to challenge. At the Fifth Party Congress and Third Great Khural (National Assembly), both held at the end of 1926, the question came up again, and the revolutionaries, instead of meeting the pressure head on, were still trying to deflect it. The pertinent resolution read:

> As to the inviting of a Ninth Khutukhtu [the one who died in 1924 having been the Eighth Incarnation], it is suspended, as there is no guidance on this matter in the sacred legends, in consequence of which a detailed examination of this question at the highest levels of the Buddhist hierarchy is necessary.*

This passage is extremely interesting. It is frequently stated in the literature that the revolutionaries prevented the installation of a new Living Buddha by appealing to the authority of an old prophecy that the Eighth Incarnation of the Jebdsundamba Hutukhtu would be the last. There certainly was a word-of-mouth saying among the Mongols that there was such a prophecy, but I have never found a text to which the saying could be traced; and now we see that in 1926 the Revolutionary Party, instead of taking the positive line and saying "there is a prophecy according to which the Eighth Incarnation was to be the last," took the evasive line of saying "there is no authority for seeking a Ninth Incarnation."

* Ya. Zlatkin, *Ocherki novoi i noveishei istorii Mongolii* (Essays in the Modern and Recent History of Mongolia), Moscow, 1957, p. 212, footnote, citing *Khozyaistvo Mongolii* (The Economy of Mongolia) No. 6 of 1926, p. 120, which in turn cites the Third Great Khural.

In 1924, following the death of the Living Buddha,
Mongolia had been declared a Republic, but the domestic policy adopted was much less revolutionary than that
of Russia; it was directed toward a state-guided economy
and the development of co-operatives to provide an
evolutionary approach to socialism. Out of this there
came what the Mongols call the period of Right Deviation, from 1926 to 1928. With the Chinese war lords
weakened by civil war, Japan not yet able to resume an
aggressive policy, and the left wing in Mongolia presumably able to call on the Soviet Union for all the aid
it needed, why should there have been a swing to the
Right?

There were in fact both reasons of international Communist policy and forces at work in Mongolia itself favoring a recovery of the Right. At this time both the Chinese
Kuomintang, later to be known as the party of Chiang
Kai-shek, and the Mongolian People's Revolutionary
Party were members of the Third International, the
Comintern, whose policy was to admit colonial and
quasi-colonial parties which were under Communist
influence, even if they were not actually Communist
parties. In China, there was a United Front between the
Kuomintang and the Chinese Communists, who were
allowed to be members of both parties simultaneously.
Within the United Front, the policy of the Comintern
was to encourage the Chinese Communists to support,
stimulate, and try to guide the "bourgeois revolution"
of the Kuomintang, but not to try to take it over—a policy that led to bitter controversy after the Kuomintang
turned against, shattered, and almost destroyed the
Chinese Communists in 1927-28.

All during these years Russian Communist policy

operated through two channels. The Soviet State dealt
with other states through its Foreign Office, while the
Communist Party dealt with other parties through the
Comintern. There were important questions in abeyance between Mongolia and China. All Communists,
and also those members of the Mongolian People's
Revolutionary Party who could be described as already
Marxists and on the way to becoming Communists, were
convinced that the farther the revolution went in China,
the better the prospects would be for a favorable agreement between China and Mongolia. It may well have
been that the Russians in the Comintern felt it would
be anomalous, and disturbing to their allies in the
Kuomintang, to encourage a left-wing policy in Mongolia while supporting a United Front in China; and
since the short-term outcome of the United Front policy
in China was certainly to strengthen the Kuomintang
more than the Chinese Communists, it is not surprising
that a parallel policy in Mongolia gave more opportunity to Mongol rightists to recuperate than to Mongol
leftists to advance.

Much more important, however, were the structure
of Mongol society at this time and the distribution,
within that society, of economic resources and control.
Western observers, looking on from the outside, have
always been inclined to a "Communist conspiracy" interpretation of Mongolian affairs. The Russians, it is
assumed, were tightly organized and disciplined, the
Mongols weak and politically immature. Therefore, the
Russians must always have had their way, and the last
four decades of Mongolian history must be interpreted
as a period entirely dominated by Russian policies and
decisions. We are therefore fortunate that Mongolian

historical material is now rapidly becoming more plentiful and accessible. This material, combined with Russian material, enables us to see that the Soviet Union was by no means committed to an arbitrary policy in Mongolia.

The Mongols were weak as a nation, yes—but vast as a country. Geographical size, poor communications, a thinly distributed population, and an economy so backward that it was extremely difficult to gear in with the industrial economy which the Russians were setting out to create—all these factors made it too costly and difficult to mobilize and bring to bear on Mongolia in a sharp, authoritative way the kind of strength which Russia then had, when all they needed from Mongolia was that it be a dependable buffer. As for the Mongol attitude, it is true that the hard core of the Revolutionary Party was not working "nationalistically" to make Mongolia more separate from the Soviet Union but doing its best to make the relationship more close and symbiotic; but it was to be many years yet before the hard core could become the solid body of the whole party. Mongolia therefore began then to work out the two lines of development which it is still following: a "Mongol" line which is guided by Mongol conditions, and an "international" line of increasingly close co-ordination with the Soviet Union. We have in the West so many who specialize on the outward-radiating power, prestige, and propaganda of the Soviet Union that we need to correct this heavy emphasis by trying to add, to our estimates of the strength of the radiation, an attempt to see how the world looked to those who, like the Mongols, were in the receiving zones of the radiation.

In Mongolia in the middle 1920's almost exactly a

quarter of the total livestock—the realizable wealth of
the country, as contrasted with the latent but still unde-
veloped resources, like mines, forests, and agriculture—
still belonged to the nobles. Almost exactly another
quarter belonged to the church (including the individual *sang* of Living Buddhas). To make the best of their
half of the national wealth, the nobility and clergy had
a high concentration of literacy—the key to the knowledge of when to act and how to act. A culturally nationalistic Mongol scholar has maintained that the literacy
rate of the old Mongolia was not 1 per cent or even less,
as often stated, and has claimed that, if we include those
who were literate in languages like Tibetan and Chinese,
though not in their own language, the rate was probably
about 10 per cent. But the point is that, however we cal-
culate literacy, most of it was at the disposal of the old
order, or those who served the old order.

This question of literacy is one of the indices which
enable us to estimate, though not to measure exactly,
one of the queer perversities of revolutions—the difference between ultimate aims and initial results. The new
laws which had deprived the nobles of their hereditary
privileges had, paradoxically, set them free to exploit
their present advantages. Lenin, far-sightedly, had advised the development of co-operatives in a society which
had no native-born middle class. But in such a society,
who could exploit the opportunity? The Mongol records
show us that the princes, and even the Living Buddha
of Urga, were quick to invest in the co-operatives. What
this meant, of course, was not simply an investment, but
a competition for control. For the investor who had
more to put in than the simple *ard* (the word that appears
in the Russian literature as "arat," "a commoner"), it

was a hedging operation—a question of how much to put into the co-operatives and how much to invest with merchants, in order to make the best of both forms of enterprise.

It may be a surprise for the Western reader, forty years later, to learn that the middle 1920's was a period of wide-open speculation in Mongolia. The Western entrepreneur was not at all taking it for granted that the game was up. A great British firm, which had pioneered in the export to the world market of frozen meat from the United States, Latin America, and Australia, and in frozen eggs, dried egg-yolk and egg-white, and frozen game-birds (like pheasant) from China, took a chance on the possibility of a big trade from Mongolia in mutton and wool. American firms, often represented by former Russians who had acquired American citizenship, were active in exporting marmot skins, furs, and sheep's intestines, which at that time, before the development of plastics, were in great demand for making sausage-casings. American firms also led in the import into Mongolia of trucks and cars, whose competitive advantage over camels and ox-carts was then just being proved. Good rural roads had not yet been developed in America, and American factories were then still turning out rugged, high-clearance motor vehicles. I can remember myself, from my early traveling days, when the "old" Dodge was the standard in frontier China and Mongolia, and the change-over period when knowing Chinese merchants and Mongols would pay more for a second-hand "old" Dodge than for a new "new" Dodge, weaker in construction, made for the good new roads that were appearing in America.

Western firms engaging in these export and import

activities partly competed with and partly made use of old Chinese firms which had in their employ men who could speak Mongol and knew the old ways of trade, credit, and barter. Such men were important in speculative trade. Russia itself, in the early revolutionary years, had great difficulties with currency and inflation, and therefore even with Russian help it was not until 1925 that the Mongols were able to establish a national currency—a reform that was not completed until 1928. Up to 1925 everything circulated—old Russian rubles, new Soviet rubles, Chinese silver dollars, American paper dollars, and lump silver weighed out on the scales. Trading profits were often realized more on exchange margins than on the "real" difference between purchase costs and selling prices. The speculative margin of exchange values gave an especially powerful leverage to those Chinese merchants who acted as agents for Western firms; they could say to the Mongols, "The old debts have legally been cancelled, but unless you pay me something on account I won't let you in on the new export and import market."

These were, it should be remembered, the years in which the world was recovering from the shortages caused by the First World War. Mongolia was only a very small part of the world market, but it shared the characteristics of that market: an accumulation of raw materials waiting to be sold and a pent-up demand for consumer goods. Under such conditions, new ventures proliferated. In 1922 there were 863 Chinese firms; in 1923 the figure rose to 1553, and in 1924 it fell to 1443. In the same years the figures for non-Soviet Russian traders—refugees from the Russian Revolution who had not been forced by the Mongols to return to Russia or move on to China—were 29, 57, and 166, while the number of British, American, and German firms rose from 5 in 1922 to 26 in 1923 and 62 in 1924. The corresponding figures for Mongol traders were 234, 286, and 635.

Of the "firms" listed, some were one-man concerns. The Mongol traders were almost entirely middlemen, doing business in a small way. The Chinese firms had the most employees and sub-agents, because it was they who sent men traveling across the country from camp to camp, selling cloth, tea, grain, flour, and pots and pans, and collecting sometimes livestock and sometimes wool and other products in small quantities. The fall in the number of Chinese firms in 1924 was probably due in part to the success of Western firms in building up trade on a larger scale. It is also quite clear that, in spite of the impetus of a successful revolution, neither the Soviet state trading agencies nor the Mongolian state-encouraged co-operatives had yet been able to bring the country's economy under a planned, administrative control. For the time being the trend was the other way. The nobility and the clergy, deprived of—or, as I suggested above, "liberated" in a queer way from—their feudal privileges, were making good use of the chance to convert themselves into a new, capitalistic middle class which had not existed in Mongolia before.

In connection with American activities at this time I feel entitled, as an American who is trying to understand how things look to the Mongols, to point out that Mongols have a distorted version of how things look to Americans. The tendency to exaggerate the theme of the "Wall Street plot" is the counterpart of the American tendency to exaggerate the "Communist conspiracy" theme. Mongol writers imagine too much when they dress up Wall Street in the wolf's clothing of an ambition to gobble up the Mongolian market.

The Mongols have made of Franz Larson a convenient symbol of the agent of American imperialism. But who was Larson? He was a Swede (he later married an American wife and became an American citizen) who arrived in China as a merchant seaman. Going ashore, he made his way to Inner Mongolia as a colporteur—a seller of Bibles and religious tracts. (At that time, many Mongols in Inner Mongolia wore Chinese cloth shoes, the soles of which were made by pasting together many thin layers of cloth or paper which were then wadded by sewing them with many lines of close stitching. The pages of Bibles and Christian tracts were often used for this purpose. They could be got cheap or even free, and for the pious Buddhist there was the added satisfaction of defiling these outlandish scriptures by treading on them.)

Larson later made his way to Outer Mongolia. Having by this time learned to speak Mongol fluently, he became an active trader. (Still later, in the 1930's, after he had been forced to leave Outer Mongolia, he was active principally as a horse trader in Inner Mongolia.) Since he did not have enough money of his own to operate in a large way, he sought tirelessly to interest American firms in trade and transportation—anything and everything that would enable him to live in Mongolia and employ profitably his knowledge of the language and his friendship with many leading Mongols. His principal success was social: he became a favorite of the Urga Living Buddha, whom he once accompanied on a journey to Shanghai—a fantastic buying spree on which the potentate from Inner Asia spent the silver of his devout subjects like, as the saying goes, a drunken sailor. The

Living Buddha conferred on his favorite the honorary title of *Gung* or Duke. For this reason Larson, as *a* Duke, became widely known in the West as *the* Duke of Mongolia—a somewhat misleading appellation.

But that was about the size of it. His ambition and capacities were limited to trying to get rich in a small way. To call him an agent of Wall Street imperialism is not only absurd but confuses the truth. In the terminology of the Communists themselves he was more like a kulak. The truth is that the real Wall Street was wary of entangling itself in Mongolia. It was interested in bigger things, and the appropriate framework for bigger things, as seen from New York, was a China strong enough to maintain its claim to the possession of such outer territories as Mongolia and Tibet, with a government strong enough to assure the safety of American investments on a large scale. The real Wall Street therefore always thought that the way to work was from the Central Government of China outward, in the direction of such fringes as Mongolia, and not, by encroachment on the fringes, to work inward on China.

To sum up: the main forces at work were in Mongolia itself. The Mongol and Russian authors quite correctly emphasize that an incipient capitalistic class was forming, enriching itself principally by trade. Since most of these new capitalists came from the old nobility and the higher, more influential clergy, and also represented a large part of what literacy and managerial skill there was in Mongolia, it was easy for them to hang onto administrative positions—and this was especially important out in the provinces, because it determined the manner in which the directives of the Central Government were carried out—and also to acquire new positions in the co-operatives and to influence the lending policy of the new national bank which was founded in 1925. This influence, naturally, was in the direction of making loans to those who were already wealthy, and therefore "better risks," instead of to poor herdsmen who had no experience in the management of money—with the result that it was the wealthy who passed on some of the credit to the poor, thus further increasing their own economic and social power. It is noteworthy that these tendencies were accompanied by a growth in the number of lamas from 87,300 in 1925 to 94,900 in 1928—a sign that the church was prospering. (The total population was estimated at 651,700 in 1925 and 709,000 in 1928.)

Developments of another kind were going on at the same time, however, and these must be brought into focus. In 1923-24, 86.3 per cent of Mongolia's exports had gone to China and Western countries; by 1928-29 the rate had fallen to 14.5 per cent. In the same years imports into Mongolia from China and the West fell from 85.5 per cent to 42 per cent—a much smaller drop. As for the Soviet Union, its share of Mongolia's exports went up from 13.7 per cent in 1923-24 to 85.5 per cent in 1928-29, while imports from the Soviet Union into Mongolia went up from 13.5 per cent to 48 per cent. The activities of the co-operative movement and of the new Mongol Bank were also growing rapidly.

What all this means is that the wealthy and conservative Mongols had taken over a good part of the position formerly held by the Chinese traders. They therefore no longer feared Chinese ascendancy; but what they now feared was the growing Soviet trade and the leverage in the direction of a socialized economy which could be applied through the co-operatives and the Mongol Bank.

In these circumstances the conservatives, of whom those who held positions in the Party and Government were called the Right Deviationists, undoubtedly did turn to their old Chinese connections (they were also accused of having connections with the Japanese), and say, in effect: "You are being squeezed out of Mongolia, but you still have 42 per cent of the import trade. Now you have got to support us in every way you can, otherwise we shall not be able to stop the revolutionary trend—and if we lose our hold, you lose everything."

The Right Deviationists fell from power for two reasons. First, the United Front in China had been broken by the Kuomintang attack on the Chinese Communists, and China was under a government hostile both to the Soviet Union and to Mongolian independence. The Left in Mongolia no longer needed to keep up the semblance or equivalent of a United Front with the Right; it could call freely on the Soviet Union for help. Second, and in my opinion more important, in spite of the fact that the conservatives held many positions in the power structure, the Left now had a stronger position than in the earlier years of the revolution. The co-operative movement, organized under the Montsenkoop or Mongolian Central Co-operative, had increased its share of the trade turnover from 4 per cent in 1923 to 24.9 per cent in 1925. In addition to many branches, it had mobile units to keep in contact with the nomadic herdsmen. It provided to the Left both an economic base and the political support of the poorer co-operative members.

Consequently in the struggle to overthrow the Right the lines were drawn in a way that is curious in the history of conflicts with parties of a Communist type: the strength of the Right was in the central organs of Party and state, the strength of the Left was in the countryside. For this reason the Left was known for the time being as the Rural Opposition. (The Mongol word for "rural" is *khödöö;* this has been adapted in the Russian literature of the subject as *khudon.*) This Opposition was led by Choibalsang, Sukebator's ally, who had been in eclipse while the Right was in the ascendant.

The leader of the Right was named Dambadorj. He is described as follows by a Chinese, an agent of the Kuomintang who was in Ulan Bator in 1926-27:

> ... most of the leaders in the Mongol People's party are Rightists who advocate union with China. Dambadorj, the present chairman of the Central Executive Committee, is an example. Although educated in Russia, he is antagonistic to that country and is strongly in favor of joining with the Chinese Kuomintang in order to reduce the power of the Russians. He is especially disliked by the Revolutionary Youth League. The Chinese Kuomintang should find a way to work with him so as to strengthen his hand.

The same author states that Dambadorj was married to a Chinese actress and could speak fair Chinese, and adds that Dambadorj said to him in conversation:

> Europeans and Americans cannot be counted upon to support the revolution of oppressed peoples of the East. Since they are all of them imperialists who have derived their wealth and power from sucking the life-blood of Orientals, how can they be expected to assist the Eastern revolution? Moreover, in view of conditions in the East, at present there is only the question of national revolutions. There is no need to imitate communism.*

* Ma Ho-t'ien, *Chinese Agent in Mongolia,* translated by John De Francis, Baltimore, 1948, pp. 115 and 162.

It is evident that from the Chinese Kuomintang point of view the right-wing leadership in Mongolia was equivalent to the Kuomintang, the Revolutionary Youth League equivalent to the Chinese Communists, and the combined association and rivalry between them within the People's Revolutionary Party coalition, something like that of Kuomintang and Communists in China's United Front, which was then still in effect. The Kuomintang leadership had by no means written off the hope of reasserting Chinese ascendancy in Mongolia.

In short, the clash between Left and Right was a real conflict among Mongols. It concerned power, but also principles and methods. It was by no means just a question of receiving orders from the Soviet Union and carrying them out. There were also proponents of an anti-Russian Chinese alliance. The decision came in 1928, at the Eighth Congress of the Party. The deciding issue was the Report of the Central Committee, and the issue was so close that it was debated for twenty-five days. It can hardly be doubted that, if the Right had won, Dambadorj would have tried to break with Russia, as Chiang Kai-shek already had. As in the case of China, however, an anti-Russian line would have resulted in neither full independence nor undisturbed isolation. It would have required a search for, and dependent reliance on, anti-Russian support in other countries. The outcome in Mongolia, however, was different from that in China in 1927-28. The Left won, and followed up its victory in thorough Communist style. Party and Government ranks were purged, and new rules for Party membership favored hired herdsmen, poor herders, workers, and soldiers, and required candidates who had more than a certain minimum to divest themselves of their wealth before entering the Party. The next year, 1929, under the personal supervision of Choibalsang, a second Communist principle was applied: not only must the Right be driven from office, but its ability to oppose must be crippled. The property (down to a certain minimum) of 669 noble families was confiscated.

From this point, the Mongolian Revolution became irreversible. Its course was set toward a future Communism. The only open questions were questions of method and speed. Even a revolution which can no longer be reversed may yet go too fast for its own success and have to be slowed down. This was what happened in Mongolia, in spite of the fact that the international setting assured the continuance of the Soviet alliance. Offsetting Soviet support, however, was the fact that China, under a Kuomintang government which for the next seven or eight years was bent on exterminating the Chinese Communists, was hostile to both Mongolia and Russia. Even more grim was the renewed forward movement of Japanese imperialism.

7

The Worst Years

FOLLOWING THE EXPROPRIATION of 669 noble families in 1929, the property of another 837 households was expropriated in 1930-31, including the property of 205 high ecclesiastical figures. And this time, ominously, 711 heads of households were put to death or imprisoned, on the accusation of having opposed the power of the state. On the one hand, the confiscations gave the revolutionaries a capital fund of livestock to distribute to their supporters, the poorest herdsmen, and the co-operatives. On the other hand, the policy of redoubled confiscation, accompanied by the execution of opponents, defines the period of what Mongol and Russian writers now call Left Deviation, from 1929 to 1932. To the term "deviation" the Mongol writers often add the terms "mistake" and "excess."

Elated by their success in rooting out the Rightists from the Party headquarters and the Central Government in the capital city without armed opposition, the members of the "Rural Opposition" returned to the countryside convinced—many of them—that they now knew all about it. Mongolia could now go straight ahead to socialism. All that was needed was firm purpose and decisive action. They and their representatives, whom they had installed in the central Party and Government organs, attacked all along the line. The "liquidation of the feudal nobles as a class" had succeeded: why not attack the church in the same way?

Capital levies and income taxes were collected from lamas, making no distinction between rich and poor lamas. Pressure and threats were used to make lamas leave the monasteries. The attackers did not discriminate between the property and power of the church—if they had done so, they could have utilized the anti-clericalism which is always latent in highly clerical countries—and the religion itself, which most of the people still regarded as their own religion, not just the property of the lamas. The result was to rally people to support the church and look to the lamas for leadership.

At the same time, small traders and handicraft workers were punitively taxed as if they were dangerous capitalists, and all livestock was taxed so heavily, without making a distinction between the rich and the poor, that there was no incentive to handle livestock skillfully and increase the size of the herds. Forced collectivization of the livestock economy was attempted without sufficient preparation. People were simply ordered to join a cooperative, often without understanding why, and all of this was done, moreover, at a time when the co-operatives, though they had been strong enough to help in overthrowing the Right, were still too thinly scattered to carry the burden of servicing economically an attempted massive shift from private property to collectivization.

With the people who engaged in private caravan transportation being harassed by the tax-gatherers and collectivizers, the state system of truck transportation was also much too underdeveloped to meet the demands on it. The chief economic consequences of this hasty collectivization were a sudden and drastic shortage of goods and, even worse, the slaughtering of cattle by their bewildered, frightened, and resentful owners. In addition, thousands of confiscated cattle were lost by being aimlessly over-driven hither and yon. The official statement is that over 7,000,000 cattle were lost. The total of all kinds of livestock had been 21,950,000 in 1929, before these great losses. By 1940, however, the livestock population had recovered and advanced to a total of 26,205,000.

The political consequences were even more dreadful. Uprisings broke out which were "a severe struggle, continuing for several months; it was the sharpest manifestation of the class struggle in our country, which reached the scale of civil war," and "many thousand" lives were lost.* It is notable that these risings were all in the west. Perhaps this was because the Japanese menace from Manchuria on the eastern frontier was already serious, and so many troops had been concentrated there that risings were impossible. As I have mentioned earlier, however, there was always a certain amount of local independence in the west; and also there had been considerable voluntary migration into the west after the revolution. Some of the richest principalities or "ban-

---

* From the article, "The policy of the New Turn followed by the Mongolian People's Revolutionary Party, and its first results (1932-34)," pp. 116-17, by L. Dügersüren, in a collection of articles under the title *Forty Years of the Mongolian People's Party and the People's Revolution,* Ulan Bator, 1961. (In Mongol.) Cited hereafter as *Forty Years.*

ners" were to be found there; but they also had plenty of room for newcomers. It may be that, after the death of the Urga Living Buddha, the higher lamas and great noble families of the west felt that the east had become the stronghold of revolution and they themselves the last defenders of the old ways.

According to an author who, as a Soviet defector to the Nazis during the war, and an officer in the Nazi S.S., is even more anti-Soviet than anti-Mongol, not only ordinary people joined the rising but "also many members of the Party and the so-called Revolutionary Youth League * and detachments of the national army. Then Soviet armored cars and planes were sent in." ** People in the region of the rising talk about it quite freely today. In a group conversation in a tent, when a date was being checked, I heard one Mongol ask another, "Was that before or after our troops and the Red Army put down the rising?" People also talk freely both about the burning of several great monasteries which were centers of the rising, and about the attacks of rebels on co-operatives, collectives, and government property such as post and telegraph offices. A young intellectual said, "It was a terrible time. I remember as a child hearing people say that if the rebels caught a woman with her hair cut short, that condemned her as a revolutionary, and they would kill her, sometimes in very cruel ways; and the lamas snatched up the babies of such women by the heels, dashing out their brains against the monastery walls." It is also part of the terror of such times that not

* This is confirmed by the Mongols.
** N. N. Poppe, "The Mongolian People's Republic," in *Vestnik Instituta po Izucheniyu Istorii i Kul'tury SSSR*, 4 (11) Munich, 1954, p. 17. (In Russian.)

a few people fight first on one side and then on the other, and then perhaps rejoin the first side. Often local and personal reasons, rather than decisions made after "ideological" reflection, make them feel that now this side, now that one is the one they should be fighting for. Russia and China, as well as Mongolia, are full of such stories.

The most difficult problem is to follow, through the maze, the thread of political responsibility. The hostile version is that neither the Left Deviation nor the retreat from it was really Mongol: the fanatical leftward drive was directed by agents of the Soviet Union and the Comintern, stationed in Mongolia, and when the drive ran into disaster it was called off from Moscow and a new policy dictated from Moscow. The record does not support this version.

The place to look for the foreign guiding hand in Mongolian affairs is in the proceedings of the Mongolian Revolutionary Party. These have been published.* They show just what one would expect: repeated references to the guidance of the Comintern and to "learning from the experience of the U.S.S.R." The policies which led to the Left Deviation were laid down by the Eighth Congress of the Party, in 1930. In the introductory summary prefixed to the proceedings of this congress, as printed many years later, the congress is blamed for having "wrongly" concluded that the revolution had entered on its "third stage," the stage of "socialist construction." On this "wrong" assumption it authorized a policy of complete collectivization.

* Decisions and Resolutions of the Conferences and Congresses, Central Committee, and Plenums of the Mongolian People's Revolutionary Party," Vol. I, 1921-39, Ulan Bator, 1956. (In Mongol.)

A Soviet writer blames the Mongols for this as if
the "mistake" had been a purely Mongol mistake *—
although, since the Mongols themselves make no bones
about constantly looking to the Comintern for directives
and to the Soviet Union for the lessons of experience,
it is obvious that the "mistake" would never have been
made if there had been strong objections from those
quarters. In the detailed proceedings, on the other hand,
there are some very interesting passages. For example,
there is more than one specific warning that in organizing various kinds of collectives the "basic rule is that
apart from collectivization by the voluntary decision of
individuals among the masses of the workers and people,
organization by official compulsion is absolutely not per-
missible," and the importance of propaganda and persuasion is emphasized. There is a comparable emphasis,
in the passages dealing with propaganda among the
lamas, on the need to get them to leave the monasteries
and return to secular life.

These details are important, in view of the general
admission that the main thing that went wrong in the
Left Deviation was the reckless use of compulsion in trying to drive the people into collectives and the lamas
out of the monasteries. It seems clear that the execution
of policy was much more reckless than the directives
laying down the policy. It is one thing to assume that
there was influence from Moscow, or even that Moscow
gave direct orders; but to assume that Moscow was responsible both for the policy and for the excessive zeal
that went far beyond the policy is laying it on too thick.
Moreover, Choibalsang, the man who had led the Rural

* I. Ya. Zlatkin, *Essays in the Modern and Contemporary History of Mongolia*, Moscow, 1957, p. 218. (In Russian.)

Opposition against the Right Deviation, was also the first to oppose the Left Deviation. This is important, because Choibalsang has always been regarded as the Mongol leader who was closest to Stalin. To assume complete Russian dictation makes it necessary to assume also that the man closest to Stalin was the first to criticize Stalin. Choibalsang's criticism was that "the over-all development of our country has not yet entered the stage of socialism, and also it is wrong to copy Soviet experience in every single thing." *

My own conclusion is that, although the Mongols do not blame the Russians, and the Russians do not blame themselves, for the policies that led to the Left Deviation, the relations were so close that the Russians must have known all about the policies while they were being debated and passed, and could have caused them to be modified if they had considered them wrong. On the other hand, I do not think that the evidence shows that the Russians imposed this disastrous policy on the Mongols. It seems to me far more likely that left-wing Mongols, overconfident because of the defeat of the Right Deviation and the successful confiscation of feudal property, drafted the policy on their own initiative. It is quite possible also that they assured the Russians that they had everything under control, and that this is why the Russians did not hold them back.

The Executive Committee of the Comintern and the Central Committee of the Soviet Communist Party did, however, intervene directly and strongly in putting an end to the Left Deviation. Some dates given by the Mongol author whom I have been quoting are interesting,

* L. Dügersüren, in *Forty Years.*

and indicate that the full story has not been told. The
Comintern and the Soviet Communist Party "rendered
great aid" to the Mongolian Revolutionary Party, in
which Choibalsang's criticism, quoted above, was being
rejected by the still dominant Leftists, by sending to the
Mongols an analysis and criticism that strongly supported Choibalsang's position.

This document was sent on 29 May 1932. It was received by the Central Committee of the Revolutionary
Party "about the 20th" of June. And since three weeks
is a good deal longer than the time required for the
journey of the representative who brought the document, could he have been instructed to consult with
Choibalsang and his supporters before delivering it to
the Central Committee? This possibility in turn suggests
that Choibalsang might have appealed to the Comintern
and the Soviet Union for help, and that they were
willing to help but wanted first to satisfy themselves that
Choibalsang, if helped, would be able to carry the day
in his own Party. If these conjectures are anywhere near
the mark, they indicate Russian willingness to intervene
to help a faction within the Revolutionary Party—which
is a very different thing from telling puppets to carry out
orders.

The Mongols acted quickly. A special session of the
Central Committee and the Central Investigative Committee was called. The Left Deviation was reversed. The
reversal was called the "New Turn." Up to this time
Choibalsang, although he was one of the two original
founders of the revolution, had been only one of the
important figures in the Revolutionary Party. From now
on he was the undisputed head of the Party and Government, and more and more the personal symbol of increas-

ingly close co-operation with the Soviet Union, including acceptance of Stalin's "cult of personality."

The New Turn is much praised by the Mongols for quickly restoring internal peace. All the compulsory measures were dropped, and the emphasis was put instead on persuasion, propaganda, and education. The new policy worked. It was an enlightened policy, and it deserves praise; but the praise should not be allowed to obscure the fact that the evil consequences of the Left Deviation lingered on, delaying progress that could have been made much earlier if the New Turn had been adopted in the first place. For example: the practice of Tibetan medicine by the lamas had been forbidden; now it had to be allowed again, which increased its prestige in the eyes of the people and delayed their acceptance of modern medicine. The willingness of lamas, especially poor lamas, to leave the monasteries and engage in productive work would also have shown itself earlier if it had not been for the persecution under the Left Deviation. Many of those who had resisted persecution now felt justified in rejecting persuasion. Perhaps most serious of all—though this is a thing that it is impossible to measure statistically—the partial restoration of the prestige of the priests blunted the interest of many people in modern secular education.

The easing of tensions under the New Turn came just in time to start building up Mongolia's strength against the now rapidly increasing danger from Japan; but, by the same token, the increasing danger caused new tensions. In 1931 Japan had invaded Manchuria; in 1932 it had set up the puppet state of Manchukuo; in 1933, in a lightning motorized campaign, it had overrun the 100,000 square miles of the province of Jehol and added

that province to Manchukuo; in 1935 it invaded, but
later withdrew from, the next province, Chahar. In
1936-37 this pressure was renewed and extended west-
ward through Chahar to Suiyuan. All of these provinces
had important populations of Inner Mongolian Mongols, and among them two important developments were
going on: direct organization of "autonomous" Mongol
areas by the Japanese, and another autonomous movement led by an Inner Mongolian Prince, Te Wang
(Demchukdonggrob), later taken over by the Japanese.
(Te Wang was imprisoned as a war criminal by the
Chinese Communists when they came to power, but was
never in fact a willing puppet of the Japanese.)

   The complicated history of Inner Mongolian nationalism in the 1930's and 1940's and the manner in which
it was corrupted and exploited by Japanese imperialism
need not be gone into here except to explain the significance of the Panchen Lama, who for some years
obsessed the security forces of the Mongolian People's
Republic. The Panchen Lama, whom the Mongols call
the Banchin Bogd, is second only to the Dalai Lama
among the "Incarnations" or Living Buddhas of Tibet.
More often than not there has been rivalry between the
two Lamas—sometimes a direct, personal rivalry, sometimes the rivalry of political cliques manipulating the
two hierarchs.

   This particular Incarnation of the Panchen Lama had
fled to China in 1924 after a defeat in Tibetan politics,
which immediately made him available both as the
potential "Chinese candidate" in an attempt to restore
Chinese influence in Tibet, and also as the potential
"Inner Mongolian candidate" to restore the prestige of
Lama Buddhism among the Mongols after the death of

the Urga Living Buddha. With the opening of the 1930's
he became potentially available in a third way—as a tool
of Japanese imperialism in organizing Inner Mongolia
and, if the opportunity looked good, invading Outer
Mongolia. He visited Japan at least once after the found-
ing of the puppet state of Manchukuo in 1932. He was,
however, no fool, but a shrewd old prelate, who saw
farther ahead than a lot of other people, and realized
that in the end Japan was not going to win. He therefore withdrew to the Chinese frontier of Tibet, hoping
to make a re-entry into Tibetan politics, and died there
in 1937. (His successor, the present Incarnation, now
represents the Tibetans who collaborate with the Chinese
Communists, and this time it is the successor of his rival,
the Dalai Lama, who has fled into exile, in India.)

As long as he was in Inner Mongolia, however, all
kinds of people were tirelessly thinking of possible ways
to use the Panchen Lama, and the Mongols are quite
right in saying that one of the possibilities was an invasion of Outer Mongolia from Manchuria and Inner
Mongolia, bringing along the Panchen Lama to rally
all devout and conservative Mongols against the Mongolian People's Republic. In looking for material that
would give something of the atmosphere of the time,
I found that I published an article in 1935 in which,
discussing the Inner Mongolian autonomy movement,
I said:

> The movement is however a danger to the general peace,
> inasmuch as the Mongols themselves undoubtedly are
> attempting to find out whether they can get better terms
> from China or from Japan and Manchukuo. One section,
> containing the more ambitious younger princes of Inner
> Mongolia, is inclined to believe that if arms can be ob-

tained from Japan, it will be possible to start a general anti-revolutionary rising in Outer Mongolia, simply by arming those of the Mongols who have not been converted to revolutionary ideas. The Mongol aim, in such a rising, would be to promote Mongol union by bringing about a fusion of the Mongols in Outer Mongolia and Manchurian and Chinese Inner Mongolia, thus making it possible to establish a separate state, analogous to Manchukuo.

There was once some talk of making the Panchen Lama the head of such a state, like the former Urga Living Buddha; but little is now heard of this.*

In an article published in China in 1935 I had of course to be careful not to say too much, because all of the Mongols from whom I got my information were within reach of reprisal from the Chiang Kai-shek security police, the Chinese frontier war lords, or the Japanese. I should therefore add now that the Mongols who talked about the possibility of invading Outer Mongolia almost invariably added that arms would have to be supplied from Japan, but the attempt would fail if Japanese troops took part—an invasion by foreigners would rally Mongol patriotism to the support of the People's Republic.

If I knew as much at this time, the Mongolian intelligence and security services certainly knew a great deal more. Agents of the Panchen Lama were slipping into Outer Mongolia and were in touch with the anti-revolutionary priesthood, and the secular leadership in Inner Mongolia also had its agents. Among both kinds of agents, there were some who also had Japanese connections. From the other side, a good many thousand anti-

* Owen Lattimore, "Mongolia," in *China Year Book*, Shanghai, 1935, pp. 35-6.

revolutionary refugees had escaped into Inner Mongolia. Among them, of course, intelligence agents had been planted. And, as always happens in such situations, a number of the agents of both sides were double agents.

The chronology must also be carried a little farther, to take in what happened at the northeast corner of Mongolia, where Mongolia, Manchuria, and Siberia meet. The anti-revolutionary Inner Mongolian leaders who thought a direct Japanese attempt to invade Outer Mongolia would be disastrous were right.

In 1935 there were some probings of the Mongolian frontier in this area by the Japanese. In 1936, Stalin made quite a sensation by saying flatly, in an interview with Roy Howard, of the United Press, that the Soviet Union would support Mongolia in the defense of its territory. This statement was followed by a treaty of mutual aid and by the stationing of Soviet troops on Mongolian soil. In 1939 the Japanese tested this alliance by making a major attack in the region of Nomynkhan; the battles fought here are also known by the name of the Khalkhyn Gol, the river along which they were fought. The result was one of the worst defeats ever suffered by the Japanese army, which admitted losses of 17,000. The Russians claim that the Soviet-Mongol forces killed or wounded about 60,000 Japanese and downed about 700 planes.*

In view of the international situation in 1939 this campaign was probably more important than has generally been recognized. If the Japanese had been successful, the whole character of the oncoming Second World

* *History of the Mongolian People's Republic* (a symposium by a group of Soviet and Mongol contributors) Moscow, 1954, p. 306. (In Russian.)

odern Ulan Bator: a block of
sidential apartments: heat and
t water are piped to them
derground from the city's
ntral power plant.

lan Bator: while modern housing
going up, much of the
opulation still lives in tents
nclosed in wooden stockades.

Mongolia's history—and its future. In foreground, the stones marking the
bronze-age grave of a Hun; in background, cars (Russian-made), with four-wheel
drive, which are able to go almost anywhere, making roads unnecessary.

In yak country, at an altitude of about 6000 feet. One of the camps belonging
to a negdel or co-operative. On the yak cart is a modern aluminum milk can.
At left, the long pole is a Mongolian lasso-pole, with a running noose at the end.

Mongol and his horse. The ancestors of both conquered their ¬y from Asia to Europe.

⌐he population of Mongolia now includes ⌐e proletarian machine-worker, with his ⌐cycle, as well as the traditional ⌐rse-riding herdsman.

A modern Mongol woman—political organizer of women's committees.

In the main hall for religious services at the Gandun Monastery, Ulan Bator.
The sloping boards are for worshipers who prostrate themselves full length to pray.

The latest Czechoslovak machinery at the "Kombinat" for leather tanning and boot and shoe manufacture.

The tethering lines where the colts wait for their mothers to be milked.

Ulan Bator's Chinese-built modern department store,
completed to celebrate the country's fortieth anniversary, 1921-1961.

A line of tents at a Mongol camp, each with its
motorcycle instead of tethered horse.

he monastery of Erdeni Jo (now preserved only as a museum),
which occupies a corner of the ancient capital of Mongolia, Karakoram.

Amphibious vehicles of the Mongolian army, taking part in the parade
celebrating the fortieth anniversary of the Mongolian Revolution.

At the headquarters of a negdel, a courier's motorcycle is parked beside posters with slogans. At lower left, the heading is "milk is gold," and the figures give yields in liters for cows, sheep, goats, and mares. Above, the figures are percentages of breeding increases: colts, lambs, calves, kids, and camel calves. At right are slogans for the careful organization of shearing, combing (of horses), collection of shed wool, and preparation of collection buses so as to waste no wool.

War would very likely have been different. It was only because they had been defeated that the Japanese consented to sign, in 1941—just before the German invasion of the Soviet Union—a treaty under which they agreed to respect the frontiers of Mongolia, while the Soviet Union agreed to respect the frontiers of "Manchukuo." This treaty maintained peace in the area until the very end of the Second World War, in 1945, when the Soviet Union and Mongolia both declared war on Japan, and Russo-Mongol forces swept through Manchuria and Inner Mongolia. The Mongols were able to field a force of 80,000 *—a very large army for a country which then claimed a population of only about 750,000.

This period had, from the Mongol point of view, its bright side and its dark side. The hostile interpretation, stated in its simplest and severest form, is that Mongolia went through several stages: independence of China (Autonomous Mongolia), followed by conversion into a People's Republic still relatively independent (in the period of the Right Deviation) of the Soviet Union; followed by conversion into a completely powerless satellite. As proof of total subordination it is argued that "the participation of the Mongols in military activities against Japan was not dictated by serious military considerations, but was merely a skillful political move of the Kremlin's." **

In Mongolia today, a man would be considered a fool

---

* A. T. Yakimov, "The Mongolian People's Revolutionary Party—organizer and inspirer of the victories of the Mongol people," in the volume *Mongolian People's Republic,* Moscow, 1952, p. 92. (In Russian.) The treaty of 1941 had been preceded by a number of local border agreements.

** N. N. Poppe, in the article already cited, p. 21.

by other Mongols if he believed this kind of thing. Everybody takes it for granted that only the shield of Soviet protection saved Mongolia from being overrun by the Japanese; and as for their part in the short 1945 campaign against the Japanese in Inner Mongolia and Manchuria, the Mongols are very proud of it. They demonstrated that their troops were better equipped and better trained than the Japanese—or the Chinese. Before this, from 1941 to 1945, they made handsome contributions to the Soviet war economy in wool, meat, livestock, and cavalry remounts; but at the same time— because, like the United States, they were not invaded, and did not, like Russia and China, suffer the horrors of devastation and the displacement of millions of civilians —the war economy was a boom economy, and Mongolia made great progress.

For the Mongols, the years in which the worst things happened—though also some good things—were the late 1930's. Both some of the good things and some of the bad were inherent in the New Turn policy of attacking the problem of the lama priesthood as an exercise in class warfare. Under the Left Deviation the attack had been head-on, against the church as such and against all lamas, with attempts to force lamas to leave their monasteries. This policy had not only made all lamas stand shoulder to shoulder, but had made the people sympathize with them and support them. The new policy was to persuade poor lamas that they were being exploited by the rich and powerful lamas, to urge those who had skills like carpentry to work for themselves instead of for the monastery, by leaving the monasteries and forming *artels* (the Russian word is used) or artisan co-operatives; to offer those who wanted to take up herding a grant of livestock expropriated from the monastery, if they were willing to form themselves into a co-operative; to tighten up the regulations forbidding young boys to enter monasteries; to tax the monasteries for every lama of military age who did not respond to the call-up for service in the army; and so on.

The key figures show the size of the problem. In 1936 there were 767 monasteries—including more than 300 which had been closed during the Left Deviation, but had revived when the pressure eased up under the New Turn between 1933 and 1936. There were almost 100,000 lamas—including an increase of about 10,000 during the 1933-36 period. They represented almost 11 per cent of the total population; the adult lamas represented over 40 per cent of the adult men of the country, and of the men of military age about 35 per cent were avoiding the call-up by living in monasteries as lamas.*

The figures not only show the size of the problem, but what kind of problem it was. No country, no matter what the prevailing religion, could possibly advance from the Middle Ages into the twentieth century if it attempted at the same time to keep on carrying such a burden of unproductive manpower. It must be remembered also that institutionally the church, committed to maintaining the prestige of religious books written or printed in Tibetan, was obstinately opposed to the teaching of the Mongol written language, and to all modern education. One can put it this way: if either the Japanese or the Chinese had been able to conquer Mongolia in the 1930's, they would certainly have started con-

* D. Dorjsürn, "Some questions of the struggle of the Mongolian People's Revolutionary Party to complete the democratic revolution against imperialism and feudalism," in *Forty Years,* p. 152.

fiscating church property and taxing church income in order to force some of this idle manpower into productive employment—or possibly, one might add, if Chinese war lords had overrun the country, they might have continued to give the church favored treatment, in order to keep the Mongols ignorant and helpless until they could be replaced with Chinese colonists.

In fact, although the Mongols themselves now, as Marxists, describe the attack on the church in terms of the struggle of enlightened atheism against religious obscurantism, it is a great help to the Westerner, in trying to understand what happened, to recall what happened in England when Henry VIII turned against Rome. In both Tudor England and Mongolia the church was vulnerable because it was wealthy. Henry VIII could reward his followers, and the Mongol revolutionaries could tempt poor lamas to form new voluntary co-operatives, by endowing them with wealth expropriated from the church. In England, the expropriation of the monasteries was part of the transition out of feudalism; it financed a new class of squires and strengthened the bourgeoisie. In Mongolia, the wealth of the church was used to finance the beginnings of socialism, without an intermediate period of capitalism.

According to the Mongol author quoted above, the income of the church and of individual lamas in 1935-36 was estimated at from 27 to 31 million tögrög, which was equivalent in amount, when compared to the annual national budgets of 1932-36, to percentages ranging from 68 per cent to 93 per cent of the national income. Emphasizing the social significance of this great transformation, the same author makes a remark that will catch the eye of any social or economic historian:

Our national working class was born in a way quite different from that of the proletariat in a capitalist country. In a capitalist country the working class was born under the rule of an exploiting, oppressing class; with us, the workers were born under the planned conditions of the rule of a people's state.

In this kind of context, Mongols call "workers" those who are employed in the new activities of both production and transportation involving the use of machinery, while those who are engaged in the old principal productive activity, the breeding and herding of livestock, are the *ard*. It is sometimes said that the Mongol society of today is an "alliance" of two dominant classes, the "workers" (*ajilchid* or *khödölmörchid*) and the *ard*, with the intelligentsia forming a class affiliated to but also subordinated to this aristocracy of the many.

But Tudor England and Mongolia are also comparable because of the tragic consequences which are part of the transfer of power by expropriation: the accusations that the expropriated are trying to make a comeback by subverting the new legality as they partly did in fact, in England under Queen Mary and in Mongolia under the Right Deviation; the reliance on foreign powers and the infiltration of foreign spies; the private revenges camouflaged by public accusations; and the sheer vandalism (we have largely forgotten how much there was of this in England) in the plundering and destruction of monasteries—the melting down of splendid jewelry and church vessels; burning or throwing on the rubbish heap of priceless art, documents, and records.

The zeal of revolutionaries led on to a kind of leftist Philistinism, a downgrading of everything religious, Tibetan, or savoring of the romance, pomp, and circum-

stance of feudal days as nothing but "feudal junk"—
reminding one of Henry Ford's "history is bunk." This
kind of thing lasts a long time, and the recovery from it,
through education and national pride, is slow. As late as
1956 a Mongol scholar had to speak out against a couple
of commissar-types who, under the alliterative slogan
"Down with dogs and burn the books" were exhorting
the people of their region to throw old books and manuscripts into the ravines, or burn them. (The campaign
against dogs needs a word of explanation. Every Mongol
family in the countryside used to keep dogs, which were
large and fierce because their chief duty was to guard
the flocks against wolves; but they were also a danger to
travelers. I have had them jump to saddle height to
attack me, even when I was riding a camel. With the
near-extermination of wolves, there is now little real
need for them; but the remoter the region, the more
people still like to keep them.) *

   But by far the most evil consequence of what is called
"the liquidation of the church as an organization" (corresponding in Marxist jargon to "liquidation of the feudal
nobles as a class") was the way in which it increased the
strength of the security police and every kind of secret
intelligence agency, and at the same time corrupted
them. This trend of development was made worse by the
fact that in the critical years, 1936-39, the infiltration of

---

* Ts. Damdinsüren, *Let Us Defend Our Cultural Heritage,* Ulan
Bator, 1959, p. 27. This is a brochure, in Mongol, containing a
small collection of reprinted articles. Damdinsüren has a long
record of quiet courage, and in his campaign against what I have
called Leftist Philistinism he named names in high places. He is
a historian of culture and literature, and has written magnificently
on the "folk" element in traditional literature.

Japanese agents and the danger of Japanese invasion were very real. Moreover, as soon as Soviet troops were stationed in Mongolia—and the Mongols needed and wanted them—the security and intelligence services of the weaker state became not only integrated with but subordinated to those of the stronger. This kind of development is inherent in such a relationship. With the next turn of the spiral, the Stalin purges increased the pressure on these services, in Mongolia as well as in the Soviet Union, to "show results," and the reflex of this pressure was a sinister corruption of the security and intelligence services themselves. Everybody now knows how this degeneration worked: by manipulating the sensational "unmasking of plotters" these supposedly subordinate services very nearly became the masters of the state, because key executive positions could only be held by survivors of the dread process of accusation, and the secret services were able to determine who survived.

In Mongolia, as in the Soviet Union, there has been in recent years a large-scale rehabilitation of the falsely accused. It is tragic that rehabilitation does not bring the dead to life, but at least justice is being done to those who survived. The Mongols call this "whitening"—which has a meaning exactly opposite to that of our word "whitewashing." White is the ancient Mongol color of divine beneficence, majesty, and intellectual purity, and in the modern language still always has an honorable connotation.

It is a sign of the lifting of fear and the healthy atmosphere in Mongolia today that one can talk about such things. I said to a historian that it seemed to me from the literature that the late 1930's were the worst years for false accusations, liquidations, and terror, and asked him

if he could tell me just what went on. "I can't," he said.
"I was too young, but you ought to see Mr. A. and Mr. B.
They were political prisoners then, and they'll be able
to tell you." I did see them—alone, and I might remark
at this point that nobody in Mongolia seemed to be
bothered by my seeing people alone. I met only one man
who was jumpy about possible surveillance. He warned
me to be careful about talking in the hotel room, because there certainly would be a recording device. I told
my wife about this, and we agreed that we would pay
no attention. Everybody who was coming to see us was
talking without any constraint at all. Should foreign
guests warn their hosts about local eavesdropping? How
silly can you get! So we not only went right on talking,
but after a guest had gone I would translate for my wife
the gist of what we had been talking about—both for
note-taking purposes and in order to compare our own
opinions.

"How long were you in for?" I asked one man.

"Fifteen months, out of a much longer sentence."

"What was the accusation?"

"The usual thing—secret contacts with the Japanese."

"Who made the accusation?"

"A perjured informer."

"What was it like in jail? I'm asking you because one
man told me that when he was being interrogated,
though the accusations put him in danger of his life, the
procedure was quite proper—no torture, no beating up,
and he was allowed to have a lawyer. But that man didn't
actually go to prison, so I'm asking you what it was like."

"It was pretty rough. No torture, but kicks and cuffs.
Jailers in those days were an ignorant lot, and they had
the old attitude that a prisoner is a bad egg, and you can

treat him as you like. Nowadays our prisons are much better, and the jailers are properly educated and trained."

"Well, when you came out, what then?"

He smiled. "I came back to the city—I'd been in prison rather a long way off—and there I saw Choibalsang, and he said, 'Hello, where've you been? I haven't seen you around for a long time.' "

"So you knew Choibalsang personally?"

"Yes, we were old Party comrades."

"Well, I met Choibalsang in 1944, and he didn't seem to me at all the intriguing or plotting type. In fact, I thought there was a lot of the good old-fashioned Mongol about him—you know, bluff, straightforward. Couldn't he stop all that stuff? Or couldn't he at least intervene in the cases of people he knew?"

"Choibalsang was all right. He was a good man. But he was under heavy pressure, and his authority was limited."

I think a foreigner is entitled to ask frank questions, but not prying questions, so I didn't press that line any further, but my inference is—considering that it had been brought out that Choibalsang had not known that this old friend of his had "not been around" because he was in jail—that the "heavy pressure" included what I mentioned above: the circumscribing of the knowledge and authority of even the highest executives when the secret services get out of hand.

So I asked my friend, instead, how he would describe what happens when a period of security stringency passes into a period of security hysteria.

"What happens," he replied, "is that things get out of the control even of the secret services themselves, and everybody is infected. Then you have not only perjurers,

and informers who are trying to make a good thing out
of it for themselves, and not only people who are trying
to even up old scores or grudges, or to get the best of a
rival, but people who are afraid that their own record
is not invulnerable, that they may have done or said
something indiscreet, or known somebody who is now
under a cloud; so they start accusing others as a way of
trying to make themselves look loyal and zealous. I'll tell
you what; I'm not afraid of anybody, capitalist or Communist, if he's an honest man and not afraid. What
I'm afraid of is people who are afraid."

I told him that, having been through the McCarthy
period in my own country, I thought I knew what he
meant.

This brings us back to the pith and core of the whole
problem—in our own country or any other: the relation
between the real danger and the fabricated or imagined
danger. In Mongolia, the tension was relieved in 1939,
when the long-dreaded Japanese attack became a real
attack and was overwhelmingly defeated—and when,
be it noted, there were no risings in Mongolia to support
the Japanese. But up to then, there was in fact Japanese
spying and infiltration. There were, especially, lamas
who thought that the cause of religion might be saved
at the last moment by foreign invaders. There were arms
hidden away in a number of monasteries. And there
were defeatists—people who thought that Japan was
stronger than the Soviet Union, and that it was time to
get ready to switch sides. The fact that many innocent
people were victimized should not be exaggerated to
make it look as though the period of terror was entirely
a period of false accusations. The truth seems to be that,
while the danger of attack hung over Mongolia it was

exaggerated by rumor, fear, and distrust. Once the attack came and was defeated, its real dimensions could be measured. People realized that almost everybody was loyal, suspicion died down, and neighbors could trust each other again.

Probably, however, the false accusations as well as the true ones hastened the final collapse of the church. The official Mongol account which I have quoted admits, for the earlier period, mistakes and excesses—treating the middle lamas in the same way as the powerful lamas, and thereby uniting them with the powerful lamas; treating the building, property, cultural objects, and images of the monasteries as reactionary and vulgar, and therefore destroying them instead of using them as they should have been used; impatiently thinking it would be easy to use force instead of settling down to a long, patient struggle; jumping from one extreme to another. It also claims, though, that the revolutionaries learned their lessons well, the main lessons being not to apply force heedlessly but to teach the people to understand the purpose of a policy, and to analyze a problem in detail before acting—and this, it suggests, should also be a lesson in other countries in which religious belief is as strong as it was in Mongolia. I think, nevertheless, that political panic also played a part, because in these years of suspicion the suspicion fell more heavily on lamas than on any other class: to get away from the monasteries was a safety measure.

Flight from the monasteries into secular life was now much better organized by the government and the Revolutionary Party than in the days of the Left Deviation. Organizers were available to show lamas and others how to set up a co-operative. Lamas who went into herding co-operatives could be provided not only with livestock from monastic herds, but with loans. Many other kinds of co-operatives were being formed—brick-kiln co-operatives, because of the increasing demand for permanent structures; transport co-operatives, artisan co-operatives, trading co-operatives. More schools were available for child lamas and young lamas.

In the last four or five years of the process, the disintegration of the once powerful church was unbelievably rapid. Of the 767 monasteries and temples, some were burned and some torn down, to use their materials for other buildings; some were adapted for use as offices and schools. This part of the "liquidation" was shockingly destructive; not even enough buildings were left to make it possible to study properly the differences between Tibetan, Chinese, and Mongol architectural principles and workmanship. There is now only one large operating monastery—the Gandang, in Ulan Bator, with a hundred lamas. It is not only tolerated but government-subsidized. Its abbot, a learned man, collaborates with the Academy of Science in Tibetan studies and the study of religious and church history. There is one other monastery, down in one of the Gobi provinces, with about forty lamas. And that is just about the lot.

What became, in so short a time, of almost 100,000 lamas? By 1938, over 5000 were organized in about 120 co-operatives of various kinds, and another 20,000 or so had returned to the herding life. Child lamas had gone back to their families or to school, and young lamas of military age into the army; I have not seen any figures for these two categories, but both were large. About 7000 were still living in monasteries. These were not ordered back to secular life, but when disintegration had reached this level the church was no longer able to maintain itself as an organized institution. It no longer had the right to tax and administer a lay population, but depended on charity, and with every additional year this meant that it was easier to live prosperously as a herdsman or co-operative member than as a monk. The remaining 7000 "practicing" monks dwindled away rapidly. But in Mongolia today it is well to remember, if you are sitting in a tent talking with a well-off, successful-looking man of forty or fifty—the manager, say, of one of the dairy herds of a great co-operative—while his matronly wife bustles about serving tea or mare's milk in silver-lined bowls, and button-eyed children crowd in at the door for a look at the strangers, that there is a fifty-fifty chance that this herdsman equivalent of the "organization man" was once a lama, under monastic vows to turn his back on this world of illusion.

8

The Choibalsang Years

For Mongolia the 1930's and 1940's were the Choibalsang years. Although, together with Sukebator, he had
led the Revolution of 1921, and although he was influential all through the 1920's, Choibalsang did not become the dominating figure in Mongolian politics until
the decisive years from 1932 to 1934, when he took the
lead in defeating the Left Deviation and substituting
the New Turn toward a policy of persuasion. He died in
1952. These dates identify him with almost the full span
of the ascendancy in the Soviet Union of Stalin, who
died in 1953.

Some months after my wife and I had left Mongolia it
was reported (*New York Times*, 1 February 1962) that
the Central Committee of the Mongolian People's Revolutionary Party had voted a resolution to take "decisive
measures to insure complete liquidation of the harmful
consequences of Kh. Choibalsang's cult of personality
in all spheres of life." While we were still in Mongolia
we had had some hints that this might be coming.

Mongol friends did not hide from us the fact that the Stalin "cult of personality" had been reflected in a minor Choibalsang cult of the same kind. "It was a bad thing to stop calling him by his name and to refer to him always and only as The Marshal," one man said. In correction of the cult it was already unmistakable that he was no longer being referred to as the man who was solely responsible for everything that went right. He was still being given credit for leading the opposition first against the Right Deviation and then against the Left Deviation, and for commanding the armed forces in the great campaign of 1945 against the Japanese, but the main credit for correcting mistakes and working out new and better policies was already being given to the Party, rather than to any individual, thus upholding the principle that in the end, even though individual leaders may go wrong, the Party collectively is the font of wisdom.

I think, nevertheless, that it would be a misreading of history to describe Choibalsang as nothing but Stalin's shadow over Mongolia. The two men were very different in character. Stalin, as a Georgian, began as a representative of one of the small minority nationalities among the many peoples of the Soviet Union. He drafted, for Lenin, the original Bolshevik policy on nationality (with frustrating consequences for the Jews, because he postulated territory as one of the criteria for defining a nationality). In the end, in spite of not being a Russian, he glorified the Great Russians above the Ukrainians, the Byelorussians, and all the non-Slavs.

Choibalsang, by contrast, was a Mongol of the Mongols. His internationalism was theoretical, though "correct" according to the Marxist canon. His nationalism was historical, instinctive, and natural. As a political thinker he was always the spokesman of Party loyalty. He fought against abuses of policy, but I have not been able to find that he ever pretended to be an ideological innovator or a modifier of doctrine. It seems to me important also, as an index of personal character, that he never immured himself in a Kremlin. To the end, or very near the end (he died of cancer), he is said to have kept the common touch, and to have liked contact with the people. He enjoyed rewarding scholars, especially those who revived Mongol history, literature, and folk tradition. He loved archery, and would appear ceremonially to shoot a round at the great national games each July. He would impulsively jump on a horse and ride off into the countryside, stopping at some herdsman's tent to drink fermented mare's milk if the fancy took him. He was a heavy drinker, which the Mongols from of old have considered an amiable failing, and when he drank with people he also talked with them; he liked to know how they felt about things.

If, then, there were parallel cults, it would seem to be more because the regimes were parallel than because the personalities were similar. As for the character of Choibalsang's regime, it was throughout one of unwavering loyalty to the Soviet alliance. As late as 1961—in order to provide Russians with reading at the time of the fortieth anniversary celebrations in Mongolia—a selection of Choibalsang's articles and speeches was published in Russian translation in Moscow. The chosen passages are heavy in their emphasis on Mongol-Soviet friendship, as in the following, from an article published in 1923:

Among us here in Mongolia, in spite of friendly relations with Russia, very few can envisage the actual situation in that country. That is why I have decided to share with you what I have seen with my own eyes.

There follow some references to economic prosperity and progress, and then:

Now a few words about the Red Army. The Red Army has demonstrated its strength to the whole world. It beat the White Guards quite a number of times... If Russia should have to go to war, it could mobilize in a week an army of several million men. All the nations, knowing this, now negotiate with Soviet Russia as an equal nation, although five or six years ago they did not even want to recognize her. Soviet Russia is the best friend of the enslaved peoples of the East. ... For Mongolia, Russia is the most loyal friend and we Mongols ought to work tirelessly to strengthen our friendship with her.*

What is emphasized here is alliance, not ideology, and the same emphasis continues through the 1920's and 1930's. There were quarrels within the Revolutionary Party, rivalries of individuals, and the death or sudden disgrace of men who had seemed to be strongly established political or military leaders; but the Mongolian Revolution, unlike that in Russia, was not riven by deep-going ideological disputes between men who, even before revolution broke out, had had individual followings and independent reputations as theorists. Unlike the Chinese Revolution, one might add, it was not split by momentous decisions between a theory of proletarian-

* Kh. Choibalsang, *Selected Articles and Speeches*, Moscow, 1961. (In Russian.)

led revolution and the practical necessity of survival by organizing, and relying on, a revolutionary peasantry.

Adjustments between far-ranging strategic theory and the urgent demands of immediate tactical action were vital in both Russia and China. These were vast countries, with immense latent strength. It was always to be assumed that, if either of them could decide its course of action on the right analysis of its own conditions and problems, it could defy the world. Mongolia, by contrast with these giants, was a country with a population of not much more than half a million—an estimated 647,000 in 1918. Its great size made its thinly scattered population only the more vulnerable to well-armed invaders. It could not manufacture arms, whereas even backward China had arsenals making small-arms, machine guns, mortars, and light artillery.

For Mongol conservative and Mongol revolutionary alike there was never a simple question of "What do we want to do?" The questions on which survival turned were, "Who is our friend? Who is our enemy?" Even for the budding Marxist with some idea of class conflict these questions could only be modified by putting them in the form: "Which class, in which country, is our enemy or friend?" Such questions were answered in one way by compromisers, in another way by men whose temperament it was to stick grimly to a decision once made.

But even if there was a distinction between compromisers and all-outers, there was a limitation clamped down on both. No Mongol could dream of being so eloquent, logical, and persuasive that if invited to Moscow or Tokyo, to war lord Peking in the 1920's or Kuomintang Nanking in the 1930's, he could change the main lines of Soviet, Japanese, or Chinese policy. The Mongols could not hope that anybody would conform to a made-in-Mongolia policy. The hard, harsh fact was that they could only choose an ally and, having done so, conform to that ally's policy.

The limitation was the same in Outer and Inner Mongolia:

> When the Japanese came on the scene [in Inner Mongolia] they favored the Mongols against the Chinese, but worked through the princes; and the consequence was that if a Mongol thought it possible to deal with the Japanese he had as a concomitant to accept a Mongol political structure in which the aristocracy and the church received foreign support. Conversely, if he thought that Japan was more dangerous than the Soviet Union, he had to accept the limitation of defending, against Japan, a Mongol state that was anti-prince and anti-clerical.*

The choice made and held to in the Mongolian People's Republic was the Soviet alliance, and this choice cannot be compared with some ideal alternative of perfect freedom and untrammeled independence. The only other choices were Japan or China. If the Mongols had chosen Japan or China, they might have found their position even more subordinate than in the alliance with Russia, but I cannot imagine that it would have been less subordinate. The record is there to prove that the Manchurian and Inner Mongolian Mongols who fell under Japanese control or remained under Kuomintang Chinese control were administered and governed

---

* Owen Lattimore, "Satellite Politics, the Mongolian Prototype," in *Western Political Quarterly*, IX, 1, Denver, Colorado, March 1956.

by Japanese and Chinese. They were given orders, and
if they did not obey they were imprisoned or shot. The
Mongolian People's Republic had—and wanted to have
—Russian experts, advisers, consultants. It certainly had
to defer to over-all Soviet policy, but it was not under
Soviet governors or administrators. The Mongolian Government continued to be Mongol.

It is in this light that the record of the Choibalsang
years must be reviewed. Choibalsang's published legacy,
which runs into a number of volumes, indicates that his
ideology was rather simple. What happened internally
in Russia was up to the Russians. What Mongolia had
to do was to go along loyally with whatever came up in
Russia, in the faith that by and large and in the long run
the Russian Revolution, regardless of crises, was on the
right track and in the conviction that the salvation of
Mongolia depended on the Soviet alliance. I think this
analysis is confirmed by a conversation that I had last
summer. I asked a Mongol what the effect of the revela-
tions about Stalin had been in Mongolia. His answer
was that, in the main, "Stalin is the concern of the
Soviet peoples. What we Mongols have to remember is
that in those times, in view of the danger from Japanese
imperialism and what was happening in China, the
Soviet Union could have decided that the safest thing
to do was just to take us over, to annex us. But it did not,
and we owe the fact that we are an independent nation
today to the Soviet policies of just those years." This
comment is not, I think, invalidated by the subsequent
downgrading of the Choibalsang "cult of personality."

The opposition in Mongolia seems on the whole to
have conformed to the same pattern. When Dambadorj,
mentioned in Chapter VI, fell from power, it does not

appear to have been a case of a losing faction in Mongolia lining up with a losing faction in the Soviet Union, but rather a case, judging from the Chinese evidence, of wanting to weaken the alliance with the Soviet Union by playing off China against Russia. Military purges, however, may well have involved personal connections between Mongol individuals and Russian individuals. When the Soviet Marshal Tukhachevskii—who, though not formally rehabilitated has recently been mentioned favorably in the Soviet press—was liquidated in 1937, he was accused of treasonable contacts with Japan as well as Germany. In view of the close Mongol-Soviet alliance, it seems almost certain that accusations against Tukhachevskii must have been widened to include some of his Mongol associates. This may explain the death in the same year of Demid, Commander in Chief of the Mongolian Army, who was reported to have died "by poisoning" while traveling by train from Mongolia to Moscow.

Stalin, Stalin's demands on his allies, and Mongolia's loyalty to the Soviet alliance bring up the question of satellitism. I think I have something like a copyright on the term, because I first used it in an article published in 1936, long before "satellite" was established in its current political usage. Comparing Outer and Inner Mongolia I wrote:

Since . . . the trend of policy in Outer Mongolia . . . depend[s] on the ability to draw on the economic resources of the Soviet Union . . . Outer Mongolia may well be called a satellite of the Soviet Union.*

* Owen Lattimore, "The Historical Setting of Inner Mongolian Nationalism," *Pacific Affairs*, Vol. 9, No. 3, New York, 1936, p. 404.

In a book published in 1955 I went on to define satellitism as follows (I quote in condensed form):

(1) The regime in the satellite country came to power
with the aid of the country in whose orbit it moves; (2)
it does not merely accept, but actively wants the satellite
relationship; (3) it could not survive without this relationship; (4) the satellite regime identifies itself with the
dominating country more than most of the population
does; (5) there is a latent opposition both to the satellite
regime and to the protector of the regime; (6) if the regime
were overthrown, the country would gravitate into some
other orbit—but still a satellite orbit; (7) the satellite
regime wants to make its country homogeneous with the
protecting country, and regards this as a desirable process
of catching up; (8) because of all the foregoing, any varia-
tions within the dominant state are promptly reflected in
the satellite state.*

As of the years in which they were published, I think
these were useful attempts to define the satellite relationship as something different from that of the colony,
the protectorate, or the sphere of influence; but something else is needed now. Standing chatting out in the
rolling country near Ulan Bator, waiting for the youngsters to come galloping in at the end of their nineteen-
mile horse race, a representative of India's Foreign Office
was kind enough to say some nice things about my
Nationalism and Revolution in Mongolia but frank
enough (for which I was grateful) to say that he disagreed
flatly with my use of the term "satellite." There are
only two boss countries in the world today, he said, the
United States and the Soviet Union, and any country

* Owen Lattimore, *Nationalism and Revolution in Mongolia,*
Leiden and New York, 1955, p. 42.

which is dependent on or obligated to either of them in some degree has to watch its conduct accordingly and is vulnerable to having the epithe' of "satellite" hurled at it. He was quite right. I had not thought of the term as an "epithet," but today "satellite," like "Wall Street plot," has become an expression used to create prejudice, rather than for purposes of accurate definition. The basic rule in such things should be that, when a term like "satellite" begins to be applied to countries which differ from each other more than they resemble each other, it should be modified or a new term used. Walter Lippmann at one time tried to get around the difficulty by referring to "their" satellite states and "our" client states, but this too is not clear enough. In what way is Guatemala, say, a client state but not a satellite, and Mongolia a satellite, not a client? Even apart from these vaguenesses, I think my old definition of a satellite would have to be modified for the Mongolia of today. In fact each of my eight points of definition would apply differently to each of the countries that are generally listed as Soviet satellites.

Even in the years when I was calling Mongolia a satellite I did not mean that either the Mongols or the Russions believed that Mongolia could find in the Soviet Union all the solutions of all its problems, because Mongolia's problems were different in many ways from those of Russia or any other country in the Soviet bloc. To understand Mongolia's economic development in the 1940's and 1950's one must first assess the nature of the country's own problems—the conditions which existed—before discussing ideologies and beliefs or the extent of the influence or control of Mongolia's neighbors. These problems had the following dimensions:

Mongolia is a large country with a small population but with vast natural resources. It is a block of territory geographically resembling North and South Dakota, Nebraska, Kansas, Montana, Wyoming, and Colorado, and almost as large. It is less desert and has more variety of climate and soil than is generally supposed. People who have not been to Mongolia, and most people who have read books about Mongolia, do not realize that it has rich forest resources and lake and river fisheries capable of large-scale profitable development. Its minerals include coal and iron in important quantities, and rarer metals like tungsten. In the 1950's oil was struck in the south and may prove out in really large figures. Early experiments with agriculture are turning out well, though there is the risk that some of the agriculture may start erosion and create dust bowl conditions. Time will tell. It is a country in which it is possible to develop an advanced modern mixed economy: livestock, farming, fisheries, timber, mining, and a diversified industrial superstructure. The question is, how is this to be done?

A problem that is run into at every turn is lack of enough people. The Western stereotype of Asian countries is that they are overpopulated and plagued with unemployment and underemployment. They have some problems that can be tackled, as in China, by mobilizing manpower by the hundred thousand, using pick and shovel instead of earth-moving machinery to dig canals and build dams. In other cases, the introduction of machinery destroys handicraft employment and thus creates problems of maladjustment at a time when the old economy is thrown out of gear and the new one is not yet in operation. If the machines are available, there are plenty of people who can be trained to use them. For this reason it is sometimes practical to buy relatively inefficient machinery, or even second-hand machinery which does not give the maximum economy in man-hours. In Mongolia the problem is exactly the opposite. The machinery is needed, but it cannot be used without drawing on the already short supply of manpower. Therefore, the best economy-efficiency ratio is obtained with the very latest machinery, using the minimum of manpower. The same thing applies in agriculture. There is no pressure whatever on the Mongols to make a change from herding to the ancient Asian peasant's hoe-agriculture: what is needed is the most modern mechanized agriculture.

These statements do need one modification. If you want to have yourself a good economic revolution, be it under Marxist or Adam Smith auspices, you must regard it as a function of education and training. There seems to be no escaping the intermediate stage in which a society that is beginning to mechanize destroys the machinery it is learning to operate, because of the universal rule that it is easier to learn to drive a car than to become a garage mechanic. Maintenance, not just "making it go," is the secret of a machine economy. In Mongolia this intermediate stage was brief. Some years ago there was a period when the Mongols had to retreat from a premature venture into tractorized haymaking and harvesting, and fall back on horse-drawn machines. Then, having mastered the rudiments, they advanced again to the minimum-manpower, maximum-horsepower standard, and are this time making a success of it. Today the Mongol who drives a car or truck is not really a member of the new elite unless he has a mechanic's certificate in addition to his license to drive.

Industrial development seems to have been smoother, perhaps because highly automated machinery was not yet available when the first woolen textile mill, the first boot and shoe factory, and the first mechanization of coal mining were undertaken in the late 1920's and early 1930's. In all these enterprises the transition to highly automated machinery (English for woolen textiles, Czechoslovak for boots and shoes) has been made only in the last two or three years and seems to have gone well.

In looking at Mongolia's manpower problem it is not enough to note simply the shortage of supply. The Mongolian society had two other characteristics not found in most other Asian societies: lack of an artisan class and lack of a middle class. There were Mongol artisans, some of them skilled craftsmen doing beautiful work, but so few of them that they should be thought of as scattered individuals, not as a class with class cohesion, recognizing common interests. The same is true of the few Mongol merchants and entrepreneurs in such activities as caravan transportation of goods belonging to others. Most artisans and craftsmen in the old Mongolia, and most big merchants, small traders, and entrepreneurs—the only people who approximated to a "middle class" or "bourgeoisie"—were Chinese (there were a few Russians, too). When most of these left Mongolia between 1921 and about 1931, including practically all of those who had any money capital, the Mongols to replace them had to be, so to speak, manufactured.

There is a great difference between a revolution whose aim is to transform the peasants, working class, middle class, bureaucrats, and so forth, of a capitalist society, even a rather backward capitalist society like that of

Tsarist Russia, and one which sets out to create mechanized and socialized farmers and industrial workers in
a society in which the previous farming practices were
only rudimentary and not even "peasant" in type, and
a working class (in the capitalist sense) did not even
exist. In Mongolia there was no history of a working-
class struggle against capitalism, no inherited tradition
of loyalty to trade unions to be overcome, no social
democracy to be superseded, no two-party or multi-party
system to be supplanted, no urban-agrarian balance to
be reconstructed. It was not a question of persuading or
forcing people to do in a new way things they had already
been doing in some other way, but of creating entirely
new activities.

Mongolia in 1921 was an extreme example of a colonial economy, selling raw materials at low prices and
buying manufactured goods (sometimes made from its
own raw materials) at high prices. There was nothing
for Mongols to export but live animals, furs, hides, wool,
and sheep intestines. Meat could not be exported, because there was no refrigeration. Salt was exported by
Chinese, who evaporated it from Mongolia's salt lakes.
Gold was exported by foreign mining concessionaires,
including an American firm. In return, staples like cloth
and grain or flour had to be imported.

Grain, for pastoral nomads, is in some ways a staple,
in some ways a luxury. It depends on the terms of trade.
Live animals are the capital of the nomad. Wool is interest or dividend on the capital. The natural increase of
the herds is either a dividend or a capital gain; it can
either be compounded, by adding it to the herd, or
realized by sale. To sell an animal or to slaughter it for
food is to live off capital. The erosion of capital by the

aging of the animals may be compared to the obsolescence of machinery in which capital has been invested.
If the nomad was able to buy grain by selling wool, he
was living on income and conserving capital. If he sold
or slaughtered an animal, he was cutting into capital.
The age at which to sell or slaughter an animal was a
calculation in obsolescence. Mongols, in the old days,
would not sell a horse to a Chinese or Russian dealer
under the age of six or seven years if they could possibly
avoid it. To retain animals in such large herds that many
of them died of old age was a kind of "display of wealth"
equivalent to "conspicuous consumption" in capitalist
societies.

For the Mongols in the 1920's and 1930's, nomads
descended from generations of nomad ancestors, these
standards represented settled habits of thought and
instinctive individual behavior fitted into the pattern
of a long-accepted society. To rebel against abuses in
that society was easy. To set out to replace the society
with a different kind of society, different kinds of ownership, individual behavior, and adjustment of the individual to his family, his group, and the nation was
difficult, dangerous, and disturbing. It was for this reason
that the contrast between compulsion and persuasion
meant so much.

Something should be said also about mining, which
was for a period part of Mongolia's colonial economy.
Over and over again, old travel books repeat that the
Mongols had a "religious prejudice" against disturbing
the spirits of the earth by mining. It is not only true that
there was such a prejudice, but the prejudice is so curious that it is worth inquiring into its origins. In ancient
times, in the bronze age and the early iron age, the

peoples who inhabited Mongolia had only very crude tools, but they were rather skilled miners and metal workers. Their society was presumably more primitive than it became from the sixteenth century onward under the influence of Buddhism, which we call one of the "higher" religions. It is worth asking therefore why a superstition which did not prevent mining in primitive times became so strongly established later.

I believe that the answer is to be found in the later evolution of the nobility and the clergy. These ruling groups had evolved through the organization of a society which depended on a cheap supply of submissive herdsmen, unable to throw off the control of their rulers and unable to escape from it into alternative occupations. The rulers therefore encouraged a superstitious fear of "disturbing the spirits of the earth" by mining; and frequently the same superstition was called in to obstruct the spread of farming. When, however, by 1915 the growth of Urga as the trading-post and political headquarters of the Urga Living Buddha made it impossible to meet heating requirements with dry cow dung alone, and it was found that there was coal near by which could be worked with Chinese labor, and when it was found that foreigners would pay a royalty for gold-mining concessions, also worked with Chinese labor, so that the control of priests and nobles over the Mongol herdsmen was not disturbed, the necessary arrangements were made without a murmur of protest about "religious prejudice." In this way mining became an activity of the colonial economy, instead of evolving within, and helping to transform, Mongolia's historic economy.

In Mongolia, it was imperative that the first stages of industrialization should be toward "decolonializing" the economy. This explains why the Mongols, unlike the Russians, were not compelled to tighten belts and load on taxes in order to raise the capital for heavy industry. The immediate requirement was light industries which would utilize the already existing and readily available resources. In 1934 an industrial combine was started consisting of a woolen textile factory, leather tannery, and boot and shoe factory, which by 1947 produced annually 163,000 felts for tents, 148,000 pairs of felt boots, 215,000 tanned sheepskins, and 173,000 pairs of leather boots and shoes. In 1946 a meat-packing plant was built and also during the 1940's a wood-working factory, lime and brick works, a power station, and a truck maintenance shop. A printing press issued four newspapers and five magazines and, between 1940 and 1947, printed 2,000,000 school books. By 1947, there were 163 dairies in operation which produced 2500 tons of butter, mostly for export.

Mongolia's first heavy industry, coal mining, was mechanized and expanded, beginning in 1932, chiefly for the purpose of serving the light industries. The first railway in Mongolia, built in 1938, was a narrow gauge line between Ulan Bator and the Nalaikha coal mines.

Plenty of room, quantity and diversity of resources, and small population must be considered together as a complex. Foreign journalists and travelers have made the mistake of assuming that the development of agriculture and industry in Mongolia means displacement and replacement of the pastoral economy. In other countries, perhaps; not in Mongolia. The new five-year plan (1961-65) calls for very large increases in agriculture and industry—but also for a large increase in livestock. In 1940 Mongolia had more than 26 million head of livestock. By 1947 the figure had dropped to 20 million, reflecting the heavy war-year exports to Russia. It then increased again to almost 24 million in 1959, and fell once more to 23 million in 1960. In that year the rainfall was only two-thirds of what it had been in 1959 (an exceptionally good year), and there was a bad lambing season. The rate of survival of new-born lambs fell 11 percentage points, and the survivals per 100 births decreased for all other animals also, except camels.

In Mongolia there is room to set mining, industry, and agriculture down at the side of, not instead of, the pastoral economy. Agriculture feeds livestock instead of displacing it. Quite as important as the supply of food for the growing urban population is the supply of feed, especially winter feed, for the livestock. This is, in fact, the only way to control the wide fluctuations in the survival of new-born animals.

The dates given above show that this initial decolonializing development must be credited largely to the Choibalsang years, although the rate of development picked up in the 1950's and went much faster and farther. For us, the capitalist spectators, this raises a flag of warning. We are inclined to think that the Russians and the Mongols, in downgrading the Stalin and Choibalsang "cult of personality," are repudiating all their works. I very much doubt whether this is either the intention or the result of the campaigns to show that men who a few years ago stood above all criticism were, after all, fallible human beings—and that, in the case of Stalin at least, corruption of character had changed a man into a pathological tyrant. I do not know so much about Russia, a multi-national state, deeply involved in power-politics, where the standards of judgment must be correspond-

ingly complex; but in the simpler context of Mongolia
I feel fairly sure that the changing standards of criticism
will result in the Mongols making something like the
following evaluation:

"Choibalsang was a great man. On the big issues, especially the Russian alliance, he committed Mongolia to
the right decisions; but he did not do this single-handed.
The best collective wisdom of the Party agreed on these
decisions, and it was a mistake to let one man alone
collect all the credit. This not only had a corrupting
influence on the man, but prevented the people from
properly understanding the collective virtues of Party
organization."

I am quite sure the Mongols will not try to evade
issues by blaming everything on Stalin. There is enough
implied criticism in condemning Choibalsang for a cult
of personality modeled on that of Stalin; it is a tacit
admission that the Russian model is not always infallible.

The new emphasis on the Party, rather than the person, is evident in an article by L. Bat-Ochir on "The
Mongolian People's Revolutionary Party as the leader
and organizer of the Mongol people's struggle to defeat
the common enemy in the period of the Second World
War." * Here it is stated that the atmosphere of emergency in the war years had the compensating advantage
of rousing patriotism. This made it possible to end the
reign of abuse and excess in the Ministry of the Interior,
which had "attempted to set itself above the organs of
Party and State." It was acknowledged that the remnants
of what had been "class enemies" had, most of them,
become useful citizens. The Mongol writer is proud of
the fact that it was possible to start remedying the perse-

* In *Forty Years.*

cution of such people even before the war ended; in 1944 there was a widespread restoration of civil rights to those who had been deprived of them.

To set this period of Mongol history in the perspective of what was happening in the rest of the world, it is enough to recall that the war era has different dates for different countries. For most Europeans, the war began in 1939, but for Spaniards and Czechoslovaks it began long before it was "official." For Americans it did not begin until 1941. For both Europeans and Americans it ended in 1945. For Chinese, however, the war began in 1931 with Japan's invasion of Manchuria and did not end until 1949, with the flight of Chiang Kai-shek and the installation of a Communist government. For the Mongols, the war years were a long period of armed vigilance, with two relatively short bursts of combat on a large scale. On a smaller scale, they had resisted Japanese armed encroachment in 1935 and 1936. In 1939, in the northeastern corner where Mongolia adjoins Manchuria and Siberia, a major Japanese invasion was defeated in heavy fighting in the steppes of the Khalkhyn Gol, and in 1945 a modernized Mongol army of about 80,000 men defeated the best troops of Japan in Inner Mongolia and Manchuria.

In these campaigns the forces fielded by Mongolia's Soviet ally were far larger than the Mongol army; but the Mongols had to remain at peak mobilization from 1939 until the victory of the Communists in China in 1949, and throughout this decade about half of the national budget had to be assigned to the armed forces. To the financial strain was added the depletion of the working force, in a country chronically short of manpower, through keeping tens of thousands of young men in uniform. From 1941 to 1945 there was the further economic sacrifice of generous contributions of livestock (including many thousands of cavalry remounts) and raw materials to aid the war effort of the Soviet Union, while the Russians, in the same years, had to cut down their contributions to the development and moderniza-tion of Mongolia both in capital and capital goods and in the supply of technicians.

Nevertheless, the Mongols continued to make impor-tant progress. Efforts by the government to protect the herds began very early. Loans were offered for building winter shelters. Stations for haymaking machinery were established, and state veterinary services were set up. In 1924 there were already 13 veterinary hospitals and aid stations, by 1934 there were 52, and in 1939 there were 15 hospitals with qualified veterinary surgeons and 330 local stations. Even these could service only 3,000,000 animals, but today there are stations in every co-operative center and state farm, with mobile motorized units which visit the remotest camps.

There was also progress in education. During the 1930's and 1940's there was an increase in general literacy and elementary modern education. The acceleration was at first slow, because the number of educated people was pitifully small. Only as teachers were trained could schools be staffed. A kind of fund of cultural energy was accumulated, however, as the number of teachers in-creased. This energy was let loose after the war—and without it the astonishing progress of the 1950's would have been impossible. "All this depends on writing," said an inspector of co-operatives whom my wife and I fell in with by chance for several days while traveling. "In the early days, with only verbal agreements, there were constant disputes about who had the correct version. Now, everything is in writing—agreements between the co-operative and its own sub-units, like the work-brigades, contracts between the individual and his work unit, accounts of work done and payments made. Everybody knows where he is and clearly understands the norm above which he gets incentive rewards."

In 1921 Mongolia had only one elementary school. By 1930 there were 122. By 1940 this number had increased to 331, and by 1952 to 426. In 1960 it was 419, a slight decrease doubtless due to consolidation. The first two "secondary specialized schools" are listed in 1924, with an increase to 12 in 1947 and 15 in 1960. The University was founded in 1947 and by 1960 there were seven higher institutions—the medical school and the higher schools for such things as agriculture and teacher training being separate from the University (which has an enrollment of about 1500). A Mongol can now earn a six-year medical degree without leaving his own country.

These figures are enough to show why the present partial condemnation of Choibalsang's personal record should not be misinterpreted as a repudiation of the whole record of the Choibalsang years.

9

Development, Transformation, Acceleration

WHAT THE WORLD most needs to know about Mongolia today is that it is an outstanding example of the successful economic development of one country by a planned program of aid from another country. Forty years ago the nation was poor, the economy primitive, the political system antiquated and inefficient, the society sluggish. Today the Mongols are, I believe, better fed and better clothed than any other people in Asia. Their housing is probably at least as good as the average of any other Asian people. Education is good, and goes a long way toward providing equality of opportunity to all, according to individual talent. The distribution of this high standard of living is remarkably equal. There are no depressed areas, no depressed classes, and because of underpopulation there is no unemployment.

All of this could not have been accomplished if the Mongols had not been a gifted people, able to respond to opportunity; but also it would have been impossible without Soviet aid. More recently Mongolia has had aid and expert personnel from other countries of the Soviet bloc, and loans, gifts, and labor battalions from China, but the main program has always been Russian, and the over-all results can be judged as an example of Soviet theory and practice in carrying out a program of aid and development.

This is of world importance. No form of international competition is more important than rivalry in programs of economic aid. The competition is open to all economic, social, and political systems. It is a kind of competition in which success creates valuable goodwill and prestige but in which, if things go wrong, enormous amounts of money can be spent with very disappointing results. International competition in this field has developed mostly in the last ten years, and it is also in the last ten years that the Soviet program in Mongolia has been most active and has had the most successful results; but since the Russian experience in Mongolia is spread over forty years, they have had thirty years more in which to learn than other countries.

Mongolia is important for comparative study because under either capitalist or Communist auspices aid programs have some results that are comparable. Economic changes have a social impact, which in turn has political consequences. New social classes may be created, as in Mongolia, where there was previously no industrial labor class, or the existing balance of interests and classes may be affected, as in India, where the receipt of aid in economic and technological development from both the United States and the Soviet Union has sharpened the competition between the state capitalist sector and the private capitalist sector of the economy.

Another phenomenon, which has an interesting history in Mongolia, is closely associated with the shift in social balance and interacts with it. New machines and techniques, when first introduced, are mere additions. They are at the periphery of the economy, not yet within it, and the men who operate them are attached to the society but not yet integrated into it. A second phase opens as the complex of men, machines, and techniques begins to change the economy and society which were there before. Then comes the decisive phase. Either, as in Kuomintang China, the new additions fail to fuse with the old elements and there is a breakdown leading to a totally new regrouping, or there is a fusion which goes beyond "old plus new," a transformation which results in a new entity ready to make its way in the world.

A transformation of this kind seems to clear the way for very rapid acceleration. In Mongolia, making a very rough count by decades, it can be said that the 1920's was the decade of addition, the 1930's the decade of modification, the 1940's the decade in which transformation began, and the 1950's the decade in which transformation became complete enough to open the way for acceleration.

It is difficult to measure acceleration in one country by the standard of speed in some other country. The newspapers frequently have stories about the rate of growth of the Gross National Product in the United States and other countries, which I am sure mean very little for the average reader. Perhaps mood and atmosphere—in themselves impossible to measure precisely—are the layman's best guide to rapidity of change. In Mongolia in 1961 my wife and I found an atmosphere of hope and a mood of confidence, which seemed to be justified by the ability of the Mongols to manage and direct new enterprises as well as to staff them with operating personnel. The stage of mere imitation seems to have been left behind. Experiment and change are going on all the time. The books we had read were already out of date, and my own description will be out of date in a year or two; but still it seems worthwhile to try to capture this point of time, because in postwar development programs all over the world so few outsiders have been present, in any country, at the moment of success. In describing what we found I shall try to use as few statistics as possible, not only because they go out of date so quickly but because it seems to me important to emphasize function, style in action, quality, even more than statistical quantity.

When we arrived in Mongolia in early July of 1961, we were excited by its transformation in contrast with the stagnation, decay, and loss of hope we had experienced in Inner Mongolia in the 1930's. The contrast between the new and the old is of course particularly striking in Ulan Bator, which is without rival the urban and industrial center of Mongolia today, as well as the bureaucratic center of national government. Its industrial growth is an unplanned consequence of the nearby Nalaikha coal mines, and may be matched when an iron and steel industry is developed in the west under the 1961-65 five-year plan. At present, with 160,000 inhabitants, it claims about 18 per cent of the total population of the country. This seemed to me to be rather lopsided for a still mainly pastoral country, but the city planners claim that the growth of Ulan Bator will be tapered off, and that with the growth of industry in other cities the balance will not be lopsided.

Rapid growth has made Ulan Bator a uniquely beau-

tiful city. Stretched along the northern side of the Tula
River, it will eventually be a city about twenty miles
long and four or five miles wide, in a wide plain almost
enclosed by mountains with bare southern slopes and
forested northern slopes, giving the landscape a variega-
tion of color and shadow. Because the population has
grown too fast for the builders to keep up, there are
still many wooden-fenced rectangles in which people
live in the old round white Mongol tents, which make
a striking contrast with the modern buildings. Because
the city is in an earthquake zone, few modern buildings
are more than four stories in height. For some reason
Ulan Bator escaped the plague of atrocious "wedding
cake" architecture which was inflicted on Moscow and
also on Warsaw in the Stalin era. The prevailing architecture is square and simple. Many buildings are a dazzling
white, but others are pastel colored, which under the
bright sunlight which prevails for most of the year gives
the city, in spite of its northern latitude, a Mediterranean
mellowness. The sharpest contrast between old and new
is in the fact that while many people are still living in
tents, heat and hot water are piped underground to the
modern buildings from a central heat, power, and light-
ing plant.

Perhaps the most startlingly modern spot in Ulan
Bator, to old-timers like us, is the sophisticated new
200-room hotel to which we were taken by our friends
from the Academy of Sciences who met us at the railway
station. It was built by the Chinese and decorated and
furnished charmingly by the Czechs in the best kind of
"Danish modern" style and comfort.

Most of Mongolia's small modern factories are on the
outskirts of Ulan Bator, the large flour mill, a tannery,

boot and shoe factory, large modern textile factory, glass factory, printing plant, prefabricated housing plant, and many others—some built by the Soviet Union, some by China, and several by Czechoslovakia or East Germany but by this time completely or almost completely staffed and run by the Mongols.

The total industrial output of Mongolia is still small, but growing rapidly, and the government plan is to double it by 1965. The following figures roughly sketch the picture of the 1950's. In 1952 there were 148 small industries with 13,500 workers and an output valued at 187 million tögrög. The state owned 37 of these factories and 111 were co-operatives. In 1960 there were 162 industrial establishments with 24,660 workers and an output valued at 567 million tögrög. Of these, 93 were state-owned and 69 were co-operatives. This rapid growth would of course have been impossible without a great deal of aid from the Soviet Union, and in more recent years from China, Czechoslovakia, and other Soviet-bloc countries. Most of the Soviet aid to industry has been given since 1952, almost all of it in the form of low-interest loans and technical assistance.

Equally revolutionary is the growth of an urban and industrial class which is still so new that the girl tending a loom or serving you at the department store counter, the coal miner and the flour mill operator, even the scholar bent over a Chinese or Tibetan text, are people who, when visiting their relatives camped far out in the country, can milk a cow or yak, shear a sheep, and catch and saddle a horse. In all the new activities Mongol nationalism asserts itself in two ways: it assumes that a Mongol can do anything that other people do in other countries, be it atomic physics or coal mining; and it

assumes that every new activity and occupation introduced into Mongolia must as soon as possible be carried
on entirely by Mongols. Foreign advisers, experts, and
instructors are needed of course at the beginning, but
there must be no industry, trade, or profession identified
with the permanent immigration into Mongolia of an
alien minority.

From the beginning, high standards were set by Ulan
Bator's industrial workers, and today in the woolen textile and boot and shoe factories of Ulan Bator new labor
is recruited only from boys and girls who have completed
the ten-year school (eight to eighteen). There could not
be a sharper contrast between such a labor force and
those of the early industrial revolution in England, Tsarist Russia, Japan, or pre-Communist China, recruited
from helpless people forced into the factories by economic failure in working on the land, or in handicrafts
unable to compete with the machine. In Mongolia, it is
not only that youngsters who have just completed ten
years of school are ready for further training on the job
and rapid promotion as the industry expands. Equally
important is the fact that the new industry is treated
from the beginning as a social complex. With the job
go rights to housing, medical care, paid vacations (which
can be arranged as collective outings, if the worker does
not prefer just to go home and visit his family, enjoying
the camp life, drinking mare's milk, and helping with
the livestock); play schools and group care of children
up to the age of eight, when regular school begins;
and so on.

Clearly the intention is to create a factory labor force,
which from the beginning regards itself as an elite, loyal
to an existing socialism which it regards as a benefit and

a privilege, and not requiring to be evangelized to suffer privations for the sake of a future ideal socialism. One result of creating such a system out of what did not exist before is that there is no trace of that hatred of the machine which elsewhere accompanied the industrial revolution, when, each time that a machine was introduced to do something that had previously been done by hand, people were thrown out of employment. (Our word "sabotage" comes from *sabot,* the wooden shoe which European workers used to damage machinery, either on the sly or when rioting.) For the Mongol, the machine is that without which a superior kind of job cannot be obtained. There is no fear of automation; the more automatic the machine, the better.

We visited the mechanized coal mines at Nalaikha, and a number of factories including the large new textile factory—which has the latest English machinery and a high degree of automation—as well as hospitals, a tuberculosis sanitarium, a kindergarten, and a large day nursery. As far as a layman could tell they were all up-to-date and well equipped.

In going through a factory I can at least get a rough idea of whether labor conditions are good or not, because that was one of the things I got in the habit of noting when I was a young insurance agent in China many, many years ago; but my experience of pastoral life was much more intensive, and I do feel that I can tell a well-run herd or a competently handled caravan when I see one. After the many months I had traveled with camels in the old Mongolia in the 1920's and 1930's, I was particularly eager to see something of the countryside and the way modern Mongolia was handling its livestock economy; so we were delighted when our historian friends at the Academy of Sciences arranged for us to make a twelve-day trip west and northwest from Ulan Bator, traveling by jeep, and visiting, on the way, four livestock co-operatives.

It is difficult to find a single word to describe the organization of the livestock economy in Mongolia today. The Mongols have specific terms for "collective" and "co-operative," but they have a third term, rendered by some writers as "collective" and by others as "co-operative," to describe their present organization of the pastoral economy. It is *negdel,* which literally means "people united together." As it is a simple word, easy to pronounce and remember, we might as well use it in English, just as we frequently use *kolkhoz* in speaking of Russian collectives. The Mongols say that their negdel have some of the features of a Soviet collective, and a few of those of the Chinese commune, but are a "looser" organization and "not at as high a stage of development" as the Soviet collectives.

Of the four negdel we visited the first was only 120 miles from Ulan Bator. It frequently receives foreign visitors, because it is a stopover on the way to Tsetserleg, a provincial capital of about 10,000 inhabitants, and Karakoram, which is both the site of the medieval capital of Mongolia and the headquarters of one of the most important state farms. The other three were far beyond Tsetserleg, and we were told that we were the first foreigners to visit them.

The first of the three, Tariyat, is less than 400 miles from Ulan Bator, airline distance, but it seemed much farther than that, because it took us three days of hard driving to get there. We were traveling in the rainy season, which in 1961 was unusually wet. For most of the way there were no made roads; tracks and meadows were flooded, and where there were no bridges it was difficult to ford the swollen streams. At one ford we barely made it by uncoupling the fan of our four-wheel-drive, Russian-model jeep so as not to splash water on the almost flooded engine. Also, beyond Tsetserleg we felt a long way off, because we drove across empty country for long stretches, seeing only occasionally a single felt tent or a low-pitched cloth traveler's tent.

This was one of the legendary campaigning grounds of Chingis Khan, and our Mongol companions recalled stories about him, and in which valley—that of the Khanui—he had said that the girls were the most beauti-ful in all Mongolia. Crossing another river, the Chuluut or Stony, which is well named because it runs through a stone-walled canyon, we came to the Suman Gol and followed it up to where it flows out of Tsagaan Nuur, White Lake, which is ten or twelve miles long. A little beyond it is the headquarters of Tariyat negdel. This is up in yak country, at an altitude of about 6000 feet, with bold but not craggy hills, forested on their northerly slopes, rising another 2000 feet. It is too cold for any agriculture except hay, and oats which are harvested unripe for winter feed. Another eighteen miles away, across flooded meadows and up and over a couple of ridges, was the headquarters of Khangai, the third negdel that we visited. From there, swinging south and turning back east, we came back to Tsetserleg by a differ-ent route, and east of Tsetserleg visited the co-operative of Khotant.

These four negdel occupied territories averaging about 900 square miles—equivalent to a square of 30 miles by 30 miles—and owned an average of 56,000 head of stock.

We were told that there are negdel which own over 100,000 head. The difficulty of keeping up with statistics in Mongolia is shown by the fact that at the end of 1958 there were 727 negdel. By the end of 1959 these had been reduced, by merger, to 389 larger negdel, with an average membership of 475 families owning an average of 43,000 stock. By the time Premier Tsedenbal gave his "state of the nation" speech in July 1961, another round of mergers had reduced the number of negdel to 337, with an average membership of 525 families, owning an average of 62,600 head, representing 78.4 per cent of all livestock. At the same time another kind of merger has begun, to make the territory of each negdel co-extensive with that of the *sum,* an administrative unit corresponding to a county. The negdel management does not seem to have taken over completely the functions of the county government, but the trend is shown by the fact that each of the negdel we visited was always referred to by the territorial name of the *sum* with which it was identified, although each of them also had its own organizational name, as a negdel, an example being "The Ray of Light." Another one that I like is "The Happy Life."

In the negdel we visited, about 25 per cent of the stock was the private property of member families—higher than the national average of 22 per cent. We were told that a family is allowed to own privately up to 75 head, the exact number being determined by the size of the family, with allowances made for old people and young children. Government officials, factory workers, and town dwellers are also allowed to own cattle which are pastured for them by co-operatives in which they have relatives. At accounting time each member family is allowed to take its dividend either in livestock (up to the permitted maximum) or in cash.

In connection with collective farming it is frequently said that people tend their own little plot of land more carefully than the common land of the collective, but this kind of thing is not possible in herding. If your family is assigned to a milking herd of cows or yaks, and you elect to own sheep as your private stock, your sheep are thrown in with one of the big herds (unless you elect to keep one or two close by, for slaughter), and may be pastured far away, by somebody else. I asked if privately owned stock carried the owner's brand or earmark, and was told, sometimes yes, sometimes no. At Khangai negdel all cattle were branded, but a nomad doesn't really need brands. Ask a man in charge of 800 to 1000 sheep to show you those belonging to so-and-so and he will go right into the herd and cut them out for you, saying as he does so, "This is the two-year-old he put in this year, this is the four-year-old he put in last year," and so on.

Each negdel that we visited had about the same number of people. For one of them, my notes show a total of over 2000 people, about 600 of them children. Counting out children and old people, there was a working force of about 1000. About 100 were Party members. As one would expect, Party members are often the kind who get themselves elected to committees and administrative jobs; but it is also true that, if a man is competent and respected, people elect him to important jobs. The Party woos such men and tries to get them to join up, but sometimes they are just not the joining kind.

The headquarters of a negdel is a little village of permanent buildings, but people of nomad origin do not yet have the villager's idea of permanence. At one negdel I was told, "We used to have our headquarters over there, on the other side of the lake, and then we moved here. Now we think this isn't really the best place, especially when the rain is heavy, like this year. So next year we'll tear everything down and move to a place about fifteen miles from here." The headquarters always has an administrative building, to which are attached guestrooms and a kitchen, so that in fact it becomes a kind of hotel, as a pattern of travel grows up within the network of negdels. There is also a school. The standard aimed at is a full ten-year school, but where a negdel is able to manage only a four-year school, its children often attend a seven- or ten-year school at a neighboring negdel. There may be a dormitory, or children may board with families living in the village. Many children ride to school from camps that are not too far away. Mongols think nothing of letting an eight-year-old child (the beginning age for school) set off on a ten- or fifteen-mile ride by himself. Other parts of the permanent establishment are a Red Corner and a hospital. The Red Corner is the community center. It has a room large enough for meetings and for showing movies (which travel around the country), and at least a rudimentary library.

We stopped for an hour or two at a fifth negdel on our way back to Ulan Bator, because we saw from the road a large new bus, a bright blue decorated traveling tent, and twenty or so horses tethered outside one of the headquarters buildings. It turned out that the building was the negdel theater and the bus and tent belonged to a theatrical party on tour. At the end of the "big city" season in Ulan Bator the State Theater and Opera break up into small parties which tour the countryside. A folk play was in progress. The episode on stage at the moment (familiar to medieval Europe as well as to the old Mongolia) concerned a lascivious monk who was trying to make time with a poor but pretty girl who was no pushover. We stood for some time at an open window through which we could watch not only the play but the appreciative audience. The room was packed, mostly with older women and young children, because it was noontime, when the men and younger women would be busy elsewhere.

Negdel hospitals vary according to the prosperity and size of the negdel and its organizational skill in getting the powers-that-be to assign a medical staff. A woman doctor told me that until recently the policy was to assign doctors to any part of the country, at random; now the theory is that, if possible, they ought to be stationed in the part of the country where they grew up and are familiar with conditions. One hospital that we visited had fifty beds and three doctors, graduates of the six-year course of the Ulan Bator Medical School. This hospital was equipped for major operations under anesthetics. It also had two cars, for visiting outlying camps. More and more, such cars are equipped with two-way radio.

Some of the families living at headquarters are in tents, others in two-room houses, some of which are built of brick, while others are log cabins. One of the aims under the new five-year plan is that every family should own both a house and a round, roomy, comfortable Mongol felt tent, covered with canvas. Looking down a row of tents and houses, my wife and I saw a sign of the new Mongolia. A little way off there was a tethering-rack for horses, but parked in front of every single tent or house there was either a bicycle or a motorcycle.

We asked a woman if we could step into her log cabin, and she hospitably invited us in. Making allowances for the square instead of round shape, everything inside was arranged just as in a tent, and none of the possessions—beds, low tables and stools, chests for storage, and so on—was too big to be packed on an ox-cart or a camel. At the back of a Mongol tent or room, where the family altar used to stand, you still sometimes see religious pictures or images, with candles or butter-lamps in front of them, but you always see a collection of photographs of family and relatives, and past heroes or present political leaders of the Republic. The latest letter from a relative is also likely to be pinned up with the pictures.

We asked our hostess when she came back with tea from the other room, which was the kitchen, how she liked living in a house, compared with a tent. She replied that she also had a tent, which she used in summer for storage. The house was nice and cool in summer, but in winter the tent was more snug, and took less fuel to heat. So as soon as it got cold enough to freeze meat the family hung its share of the autumn slaughter in the house, and moved into the tent. The more "modern" Mongols are, the more likely they are to say that tuberculosis and respiratory diseases go with the tent life. I think they get this idea from the Russians, and that it is wrong. A Mongol tent is easily kept warm in winter, easily ventilated, and not drafty if properly snugged down along the ground line. I have not lived in Outer Mongolia in winter, but in the old days in Inner Mongolia I often had a cold when living in houses, and never had one when living in tents.

In developing the negdel form of collective or co-operative the Mongols have now had a lot of experience, ranging from the disastrous headlong approach of the Left Deviation through the years of the "persuasive" policy of the New Turn, to the post-war years in which they have been able to budget more money for special training courses for co-operative managers, accountants, and the like.

As late as 1947, 99 per cent of the cattle were privately owned. There were about 100 co-operatives, but only 0.2 per cent of the cattle were owned by them, and the other 0.8 per cent were owned by state farms and stations. By 1957, 75 per cent were still in private hands and 678 co-operatives owned 22 per cent. It was only about 1958-59 that they moved back to a policy of compulsion, and the last hold-out private-enterprise herdsmen were ordered to join co-operatives. When they did so, there was no question of compensation, based on the number of livestock they owned; they just turned in their stock, and joined.

By the time this happened, however, the private herdsmen were more than ready to join. The co-operatives were flourishing, and the people who had stayed out were "cattle-poor," as we speak of a man being "land-poor" when he has a lot of land, has to pay taxes on it, but does not have the money capital to develop it properly. Most of those who had stayed out of the co-operatives were, naturally, rather well off; but this meant that they had to hire shepherds. As co-operatives became more profitable, poor people wanted to join them instead of working for private owners—and here is the twist to this story. With Mongolia's universal labor shortage, and the co-operatives now having plenty of cattle, the co-operative managers were more in need of new members than of additional cattle. Rich men were being turned away, because they had too many livestock, of which the co-operative had more than enough, and too little manpower, of which the co-operative was short. Thus, when co-operatives were finally made fully compulsory, it was in many cases just as much an order to the co-operatives to admit new families as it was an order to the hold-out families to join.

It is quite clear that the Mongol planners are aiming to convert the livestock economy from a nomadic structure to something like a ranch structure, with most of the people sedentary most of the time. They will not be able to do this for a good many years, because of the same old story of labor shortage. Small numbers of people handle large herds. The larger the herd, the more frequently it has to be moved, because the greater the concentration of animals the more they trample the pasture, destroying the herbage. The present system is complicated, but still rather closely connected with the traditional system. Two to four "big" moves are made each year, depending on the type of country. This is as it was in the old days; but there is now more specialization and a much greater diversity of subsidiary activities. Since the camps through which the many activities of a co-operative or negdel are dispersed are usually miles apart, there is a strong emphasis on individual initiative and willingness to take responsibility.

Specialization ramifies in many directions. First of all, there is the separation of the various kinds of animals, in order to place each kind on the pasture most suited to it. Sheep are herded the farthest away from other animals, and herds of sheep are usually much bigger—

not less than 800 to 1000—than other herds. They graze on a wide front, cropping the grass very short. Goats used to be herded along with sheep, but now seem to be herded separately. They are commercially important for their underwool ("cashmere") and for their skins. Sheep account for 52 per cent of the total livestock, but I was rather surprised to find that goats account for as much as 25 per cent.

A further degree of specialization is to separate mothers and their young from other animals. This is beneficial for all animals, and commercially important for dairying activities. Cows and yaks, which for some reason never seem to be separated statistically, make up only 8.3 per cent of the livestock population, but that comes to nearly two million. There is now enough cow's milk so that few people continue to drink sheep's milk, as they used to do in the old days; there is plenty of cheese, though mostly of Mongol kinds for which it would be difficult to find a foreign market, and an important export trade in butter, which goes to the Soviet Union.

A dairy herd is called a *ferm*—using the Russian word, which the Russians in turn probably borrowed from French or German rather than from English. One such ferm which my wife and I visited consisted of fifteen families milking 200 cows, yaks, and *hainag* or cross-breds. They made four kinds of cheese, and delivered part of their milk to a butter-central, which also collected from other ferms. A specialized camp of this kind engages in elaborate exchanges of its milk and cheese with other camps, all of course being within the same negdel organization. The butter-central—also belonging to the negdel—had two churns, one worked by hand power and one run by a little gasoline engine, which had been presented to the negdel by the state, as a reward for good quality and quantity of production. Language is often psychologically interesting, and I noticed that, when Mongols speak of receiving an order from a government bureau, they use a term which means "the place of control"; but when the manager of this butter-central spoke of the engine presented by the government, he said, proudly, that it was "the gift of the Nation"—using a word that also means "people" and even, anciently, "tribe."

Another kind of milking unit is the herd of mares, and this brings in another illustration of the psychology of language. For cows, you may use a foreign word like *ferm,* but for mares nothing but the proud old traditional words will do. If you are asking your way to the herd of mares, you ask, "Where have they captured the mares?" Mongols believe that mare's milk, which is always drunk fermented and about as strong as beer, not only tastes better than anything else in the world (and I agree), but is practically an elixir of life. Russian doctors have taken over from the Mongols, and from the Kazakhs and Kirghiz of Central Asia, the belief that it is both preventive, and curative in the convalescent stage, for tuberculosis and for such modern industrial diseases as silicosis. The great coal mines at Nalaikha, which fuel the power plants and industries of Ulan Bator, have their own herd of 30,000 mares, and every miner is entitled to his ration.

We visited a herd of 600 mares, a unit belonging to a negdel. The man in charge, heavy-shouldered, thick-bodied, short-legged, had concentrated in him, I thought, more of the old Mongolia than any other one man we met. He gave the impression of not particularly caring

who ran Mongolia, as long as he was allowed to handle
his herd the way it ought to be handled—and of thinking rather well of the present government, because it let
him do just that. His mother, eighty-seven years old,
belonged to the past and was not ashamed of it. She was
a *chavgants,* a woman who after the change of life has
shaved her head and is considered a "female lama"—
that is to say, something like a nun, but still living in
the family and tending the family altar.

A Mongol cow does not produce more than 600 liters
of milk a year—more in small milking units, where
more attention can be given to the individual cow.
Higher yields are expected in the future, as the Mongols
succeed in developing special milk breeds and meat
breeds; but for the present the yield is low, as compared
with Western and American standards. In America an
ordinary dairy herd—not the highest quality—will yield
as much in a month as Mongol cows do in a year. The
explanation is that if our dairy herds were all pastured
on the open range, with a North Dakota winter climate,
no barns, few shelter corrals, little hay, and no oil-cake
feed, the yield would be more like that of Mongolian
cows. This is one of the best illustrations of the fact that
increasing agriculture in Mongolia does not threaten the
livestock breeders but is welcomed by them and beneficial to them. Severe climatic conditions, lack of shelters,
and the fact that the spring storms are the worst of the
year also account for the fact that large numbers of
lambs, kids, colts, and calves are lost at birth or survive
for only a few days—another argument for changing from
full nomadism to something like a ranch type of herd
management.

In comparison, the yield of a mare is startlingly large

—three to five liters a day; though for a much shorter milking season than a cow. This yield depends very much on whether the pasture is lush or dry, and the number of times a day a mare is milked depends also on the pasture. To get the best yield, a mare must be milked very fast, for only a few moments at a time. On the rich pastures of the Khangai provinces she can be milked up to twelve times a day; on the drier pastures of the Jabkhan region, also in western Mongolia but south of the Khangai region, only about eight times a day. In either case, getting a supply of the much longed for mare's milk makes a severe demand on Mongolia's short-supply manpower.

In a milking herd of mares, the foals are tethered in lines to cords pegged down along the ground. At milking time, men and boys round up the mares on the open range and drive them back toward the tethering lines. As each mare is caught, a man or boy brings her own foal up and holds it alongside her, to induce her to give milk; a woman does the milking. In the old days, the Mongols kept milk in containers of wood or leather; now they use aluminum. They have also zealously adopted the idea that everything connected with milk must be clean and sanitary. For milking, making cheese, or working in a butter-central, a white gown must be worn.

In the old Mongolia the employment pattern was extremely uneven. Tens of thousands of monks sat idle in the monasteries, but at the same time children, since they did not go to school, were available for most of the routine work of herding. Untold working hours—mostly the work of women and children—were spent in trudging around the steppe to pick up dry cow dung and camel dung for fuel. When, in summer, riding through an empty landscape, you came across an enormous stack of dry cow dung, squared at the sides and plastered on top to keep out the rain, you knew that someone had prepared it for his winter camp. Cow dung is good fuel, but in the busy Mongolia of today nobody has the time to go out and gather it if wood or coal is available. An urban concentration like Ulan Bator, with its 160,000 people, would be impossible without its nearby coal mine, and in the co-operatives going to the forest for fuel (or building timber) is an important job that somebody has to do. To be done efficiently, it has to be organized.

This, and all kinds of other intermittent work like shearing, driving herds to a slaughter-point or export-point, putting up a building, rough-and-ready road-making, or bridge-building, is done by a *birigad,* in which everybody will recognize the international word "brigade." A birigad is a task-force organized for a particular job and disbanded when the job is done. Even though the men who work on this job belong to the co-operative, they sign a contract for that particular job, and the "labor-days" credited to each man go down in the accounts. Estimating the cost, checking over the work-lists to see who can be spared for assignment to a particular birigad, and agreeing on the incentive bonus for above-standard work or completing the contract ahead of time represent a concept of work and of the relation of the individual to the group, and a complexity of organization quite unknown in the old Mongolia. This is a real part of the revolution which changes the character of a society.

Another part of the revolution is the complex of activities which gear the co-operatives into the national economy. All of these are traceable to Russian originals, but all have peculiarities which derive from Mongolian

conditions. First of all, in a vast country still short of
the rail and truck transportation it will someday have,
manpower and transportation cost must be conserved
as much as possible in delivering the output of the co-
operatives to the state trading agencies, wool-washing
plant, textile mill, meat-packing plant, and so on. This
is done in the following way: The co-operative organizes
its own birigad for short-haul delivery to an intermediate
point, the "preparation" station—what we would call a
processing station. Here wool, hair, manes, tails, hides,
furs, and so on are sorted, graded, given a preliminary
or intermediate cleaning if needed, and turned over to
the trucks of the state transportation agency for long-
haul delivery.

Some small-scale haying is done by the co-operatives
themselves with horse-drawn machines, but large-scale
haying, ploughing, and harvesting are done by contract
with a special state agency, the MTS or Machine and
Tractor Stations. As in Russia these stations developed
out of a double need—the shortage of machines and the
need, in an under-mechanized country, to train men in
skilled maintenance as well as in simply driving the
machines. I might add that in my opinion pastoral
nomads, though most people think they are more "primitive" than farmers, master the machine more quickly
than peasants do, because they know that maintenance
is all-important. Horsemanship is not just galloping
across the country; it means knowing how to look after
the horse, and, if you are going to move livestock on a
long drive, knowing what to do with the lame animal
is good, but it is better to see to it that the animals don't
go lame.

In 1956 there were only four MTS, serving fifteen

negdel. By 1960 there were 36, serving 180 negdel, many of them bigger negdel, because of the mergers that I mentioned previously. Serving fewer but bigger negdel greatly increases efficiency in the use of machinery. With the ploughing of enormous additional tracts of virgin land, the importance of the MTS will be still further increased. In 1940 only 66,000 tons of hay were cut, and the grain harvest was 14,900 tons, but by 1960 production figures were about 1,477,000 tons of hay and 256,000 tons of grain. In 1957 there were 199,000 acres of ploughed land, which by 1960 had risen to 6,372,000 (a figure which the government plans to triple by 1965). The planned new ploughing has already begun, with the receipt in the last two years of several thousand more tractors from the Soviet Union.

This tendency toward delegating special functions to special units is balanced by a tendency, within the negdel, to do more things for themselves. As they prosper, and the number of trained mechanics in their membership increases, they invest in their own trucks, cars, and four-wheel-drive jeeps. Even within a negdel's own domain, a short-haul truck releases men from the work of driving strings of ox-carts or leading caravans of camels.

Again following the Soviet example, the Mongols have state farms, on which the labor force are wage-earners, not profit-sharing members. State farms are multiple-activity centers of experiment, innovation, and technical improvement. Instead of depending on the MTS, each farm has its own park of machinery, and the farms engage in rainfall farming and irrigated farming, in which they experiment with food crops, and in livestock breeding, in which they experiment with cross-breeding with imported stocks and the improvement of native stocks by selective breeding. It is obvious that the danger of running into heavy erosion and dust-bowl losses in ploughed agriculture is to an important degree insured against by the operations of such farms, which are directly under the state and its scientific institutions, and in a position to report promptly the development of an adverse trend.

In 1960 there were 35 state farms, with 480,000 acres under cultivation—77 per cent of the total crop land of Mongolia. In livestock, they go in for quality more than quantity. They own no more than 475,000 head, as against the 17,000,000 head in the co-operatives and 5,400,000 head privately owned by negdel members and industrial workers and government employees. The importance of the work done on state farms is shown by the fact that they invariably rank ahead of the co-operatives in such things as rate of breeding increase, weight of wool per sheep, and so on. It was on a state farm, after years of experiment, that a new breed of sheep was stabilized, the Orkhon, which produces more meat and more and finer wool than any of the old Mongolian breeds. State farms are also responsible for introducing artificial insemination.

It is possible that artificial insemination will have an especially marked effect in horse-breeding. The traditional Mongol practice is to give each stallion a band of 15 to 20 mares. He herds them out on the open range and regularly brings them to drink at a well or stream in what he has learned to consider "his own" territory. "A stallion leads his mares to water and drives them away from it," was the old Mongol saying, and this was true; the stallion comes first to the water, stands by while his mares drink, then drinks himself, then herds his mares back to the range. But a difficulty with stallions is that as they get older they get more savage and dangerous. Therefore the Mongols tended to geld them rather young and replace them with new, still younger stallions, which meant that most colts were sired by stallions not fully matured. Artificial insemination makes it possible to wait and select the stallions which have shown the best qualities.

Outwardly, in spite of new agriculture, industry, and urbanization, many of the characteristics of the old Mongol life seem unchanged. In reality, the whole society has been transformed—even the "old" pastoral economy. Up to 1921, 8 per cent of Mongol families belonged to the aristocracy and owned 43.5 per cent of all livestock, with an average of 2370 head per family. The 92 per cent of all families who were commoners owned an average of barely 50 head per family, and of course there were many families who had no stock at all. Today, in one co-operative of 2000 people owning 80,000 head of stock the average holding would be 40 head—not per family but for every man, woman, and child. Government statistics for all co-operatives record an average of 52 head per member (everyone over 16), plus 15 privately owned head per member. In addition, each family has a cash income for the work done in herding, on "birigad" jobs, and so on, the various kinds of work being equated with each other by the elaborate Soviet-style "labor-day" form of accounting.

In the Mongolian countryside the transformation and acceleration mentioned at the beginning of this chapter are in some ways not so obvious as they are in Ulan Bator; but they are there, and not only in the physical,

tangible prosperity of more and better food, better
clothes, neater, solider tents and houses. They are also
reflected in the people's pride in their achievements,
their pleasure in showing foreigners what they have and
in talking about better health, education, and recreation.
A number of recent writers about China describe an
atmosphere of grim, unremitting toil and effort. That is
not the atmosphere in Mongolia. The Mongols act like
people who are confident that they now have the knack
and the know-how to tackle any problem that may come
along, and so are entitled to take the afternoon off now
and then and go for a picnic.

In such an atmosphere it is not surprising that the
overwhelming majority of Mongols—not just members
of the Party and the Government—consider the relationship with Russia a huge success; they also have great
confidence in their own Party and Government; they
think that their country is on the right course; they like
it the way it is; they think that the present is much better
than the past; and there is a buoyant optimism about
the future—as in America in the late nineteenth century.

It is also true, and underlines the importance of not
using blanket terms that muffle differences more than
they reveal similarities, that what I have just said about
Mongolia applies only to Mongolia. Something different
would have to be said about every other country that is
under a government controlled by a Communist Party.
One has only to start calling the roll of names alphabeti-
cally: Albania, Bulgaria, China—why go further? And
who knows what distinctions the ordinary person in
North Korea makes when he compares his country's relationship to the Soviet Union and to China?

Mongolia, like any other country, also has its historical heritage. Even the uniformity of Marxist thinking and the command of a Communist Party to think of all other Communist-ruled countries as "socialist brothers" cannot make history in a hurry. In Poland there is a deeply rooted folk tradition that "the Russians—and the Ukrainians, and the Byelorussians, and the Jews and the Germans—are not our kind of people." Old hatreds and suspicions of this kind are hard to eradicate. In Mongolia there is one old tradition that you can always get along with the Russians, and another old tradition that the Chinese are enigmatic and somehow menacing, and you either have to knuckle under to them or stand them off. Relations between Mongolia and China are good. Mongols speak enthusiastically about the fact that having a Communist China on their southern frontier makes it no longer necessary to keep up a big army. They are cordial about the Chinese labor battalions which do so much of the building and road-making in Mongolia. They would, I am sure, be distressed if they found themselves in an "Albanian" situation between Russia on one side and China on the other. But the fact remains that man-to-man relations between Mongols and Russians are easy, while friendship between Mongols and Chinese is something that has to be worked at.

The slogan of "socialist brotherhood" need not be accepted at full face value. There are three Great Powers in the World (here I modify the opinion of my Indian friend)—America, Russia, and China—and there is something about being a Great Power that makes a country behave like a Great Power, regardless of the official ideologies of Marxism and capitalist democracy. Major Soviet and Chinese policies are always announced in ideological terms, and it is well to try to master and understand these terms; but it is also prudent always to try to analyze a Soviet or Chinese policy in terms of the Great Power interests involved. I can illustrate this. A Russian said to my wife—this was in 1960, and the speaker was a Soviet expert on China—"In the Chinese book, you Americans are their worst enemies and we Russians are their best friends. Now they see their best friends trying to work out some way of peaceful co-existence and competition with their worst enemies—and they don't like it."

I have emphasized that the Mongols have their own history and their own heritage. So do the Chinese; and in this heritage no tradition is more important than the belief that the Chinese are *the* civilized people of the world and that therefore the Chinese solution of a problem is always the best one. This tradition has to be taken seriously. It has more historical justification than the boasts of many another country. It is possible that, animated by it, the Chinese will catch up with the Soviet Union before the Russians catch up with the West. The Chinese learn fast. Every foreigner who did business in China in the old days knew that a very large number of his employees soon became competent to handle jobs two levels or three levels above the one they were being paid for.

This readiness to step up into a higher rank is related to the fact that China has the oldest uninterrupted, homogeneous culture in the world. Because of this long continuity Chinese society was saturated with the higher intellectual qualities of its own culture. A Chinese might be poor, ignorant, and at the very bottom of the society which had evolved that culture, but he knew what culture was, and he thirsted for it. The Chinese peasant, if he had luck and got a little bit ahead, tried to break through upward, into the "scholar-gentry," and he usually succeeded. If it was too late to get there himself, he got his sons there, or his grandsons.

The Mongols know a lot about the Chinese—much more than we do. They have been in side-by-side contact with them for many centuries. On my last day in Mongolia we drove past a Chinese construction job. My companion, a scholar, began talking with the driver about the Chinese. The driver was just as much at home in that subject as the intellectual. They agreed that the Chinese are the wonder people of the world. They can make out in any climate and in anybody's country. They can do the most brutal heavy labor, the finest handicraft, the most delicate art. Anything they do is planned and methodical: they have thought it out first. And they stick together.

I have said before that in recent centuries the Mongols have felt more affinity for the Russians, specifically the Siberian forester-farmer-herdsman Russians, than for Chinese merchants and peasants. This does not mean that today they think of the Soviet Union and Communist China in either-or terms. I have seen it suggested that the Mongols might want to go along more closely with China than with Russia, because the Chinese are Asians and the Russians are not. This is an illusion. The Mongols do not particularly think of themselves as Asians, and never did. There is absolutely no evidence, from the days when they were conquerors, that the Mongols thought of themselves as conquering or uniting "Asia." They just defeated everybody they came across, and that included Russians, Poles, Hungarians. As far as "Asia" meant anything to them in the past, it meant the lands of the peasant cultivators, and the Mongols were not peasants. They were horsemen, herdsmen, *nüütel uls*—people on the move.

With an independent history of their own, I believe that the Mongols today do not want to have to choose between the Soviet Union and Communist China. Why should they want to compete antagonistically, with one side against the other side? Of course they repeat the usual slogans of a competition with capitalism, in which capitalism will be defeated, but what they really want is friendly relations and trade even with the capitalist countries, as long as it is understood that they are interested in new friends in addition to old friends, not instead of old friends, and are not looking for a chance to break away from their Soviet alliance.

As things now stand, they are closer allies of the Russians than of the Chinese, and have been for a long time. What they want most, I am sure, is continuing cordial relations with both their giant neighbors, combined with a nationalism at home, whose ambition it is to fill Mongolia with a rapidly growing Mongol population, and to raise the material and intellectual level of that population to a proud place in the world culture.

As for the rest of the world, there is more eager curiosity about America than about any other country. Many Mongols talked to me and my wife about the possibility of diplomatic relations with the United States, and cultural and economic relations, too, and always enthusiastically. They are convinced that they can learn a lot from us, not only in science, technology, and industry but also in their own special historic occupations, livestock-breeding and range management.

The Mongols have been lucky so far in the adjustment the Russians and the Chinese have made between ideology and Great Power interests. Russians and Mongols know as well as the Chinese themselves how decisive the victory of the Chinese Communists was. They know that in spite of present difficulties and setbacks, nothing can now stop the Chinese from becoming one of the greatest nations of the world—a leading nation in thought, invention, discovery, as well as power. For the time being it would seem that the Soviet Union and China, tacitly acknowledging their grave conflicts of interest elsewhere, have agreed that things would only be made worse by rivalry in Mongolia. Whatever happens, increased communications with each other are an imperative need for both the Soviet Union and China, and it is better to have those communications run through a rapidly developing Mongolia than across a backward waste. There is so much to be done in development economics that the aid programs of the two countries in Mongolia can be made complementary instead of competitive.

10

Horseback Is All Right

MONGOLIA HAS MORE THAN 6000 students in higher institutions, and it is claimed that in ratio to total population this establishes a standard higher than that of West Germany, not to mention a number of other countries less industrialized and advanced than West Germany—Italy, Japan, Turkey, Pakistan, and Iran. Doubtless this is true, but Communists, like others, like to present statistics in the manner most favorable to themselves. This high general average does not mean that Mongolia comes anywhere near to being in the same class as West Germany in discovery, invention, and advanced research; but it does mean that intellectual life in Mongolia is exciting, diverse, and vigorous. The Mongol intellectual is a man who is confident that there is nothing in the world of the mind that he cannot tackle, and invariably, in my experience, the very highly specialized man has interests that range far and wide beyond his special subject.

It is common to plunge into the description of such phenomena of rapid development with picturesque journalistic phrases about the descendants of Chingis Khan's savage warriors now flying jet planes. This is altogether wrong and misleading, because it exaggerates the barbarousness and ignorance of the Mongol past. Mongol revolutionaries have themselves contributed to this distortion, because it was fashionable at one time to decry and denigrate the whole past in order to make the revolutionary present look brighter and the future more promising. The truth is that Chingis Khan himself, though he never learned to read and write, not only respected men of brains and knowledge but knew how to use them. From the moment their conquests brought them into contact with the cultures of China and Iran, and more distantly the cultures of India and the Arabs, the Mongols began to develop what can fairly be called an intelligentsia, partly within the ruling class and partly in the service of the ruling class, and Khubilai Khan, grandson of Chingis, was probably as well educated and cultured as any European sovereign of his time.

It is possible that the origins of a higher Mongol culture should be set even earlier. At the beginning of the thirteenth century, under Chingis Khan, the Mongols borrowed the alphabet (of Semitic origin) used by the Uighur Turks. It is usually assumed, simply because nothing written has been found, that nothing was written in Mongol before this time. An eminent Mongol scholar, Ts. Damdinsüren, suggests, however, that, since it can be demonstrated that in the thirteenth century there was already a "literary" Mongol different from the vernacular, the Mongols must by then have had some way of writing things down for several hundred years. The suggestion is a striking one and a reminder that in the eighth century the Orkhon Turks in central Mongolia had a runic writing, and in the tenth and eleventh centuries the Khitan (Liao) Dynasty and in the twelfth century the Jurchid (Chin) Dynasty, both of which had considerable power in Mongolia, each had its own system of writing. Any of these systems could readily have been adapted for writing Mongol. The Khitan language can be regarded as an eastern neighbor and variant of the Mongol language. In addition, it can be pointed out that Chingis, an eastern Mongol, learned of the Uighur writing when he conquered the western Mongols—who may have been using it for a long time. The trouble is that nothing written in the Mongol language, in any form of writing, has survived from earlier than the thirteenth century.

After the fall of their empire, in their wars among themselves and the wars in which they were conquered by the Manchus, there was a lamentable loss of manuscripts and records. This period gives a somewhat misleading impression of a Dark Age, a relapse into barbarism. There was a relapse, but not a total relapse. More than a hundred years ago, in the introduction to his Mongol-Russian-French Dictionary, the great Kowalewski, a political exile from the Russian-ruled part of Poland who later became thoroughly Russianized, paid tribute to Mongol scholarship. He notes that the original stock of the Mongol language is the vocabulary of herdsmen and hunters. With the introduction of Buddhism and the translation into Mongol of Tibetan and Sanskrit texts, "nomadic expressions had to be adapted to abstract ideas." The priestly translators, he says, "conscientiously fulfilled their task, rarely borrowing foreign words and making every effort to provide expressions of their own when they could do so without altering the text."

Another intellectual influence came in with the translation of some of the Chinese Confucian classics, and also—even in the first half of the nineteenth century—Western ideas had begun to have some influence through the translation of Christian texts and proselytizing literature, and of scientific knowledge "current among the Asian peoples in contact with Europe." There were, it should be added, Mongols who wrote and wrote well in Tibetan, Chinese, and Manchu, as well as in Mongol, and by the end of the century there was an increasing flow of knowledge of all kinds from Russia, in which Buryats were influential.

In a cultural tradition, quality is all-important. Once it has attained a certain level, a culture may be overwhelmed by a long period of distress, poverty, and ignorance and yet lie dormant like a seed, ready to sprout again when times get better. That is certainly what has happened in the history of the Mongol culture, which has made a superb recovery. Its vehicle, the Mongol language, having made the transition centuries ago from being a folk language to becoming a language adapted to any kind of sophisticated use, has a seasoned vitality. It is a beautiful language. The Mongols love it as the French love their language, and like the French they are jealous of it and like to hear it well spoken. It has a rich heritage of epic poetry, folk poetry, folklore and proverbs, and a varied repertory of style—the archaic, the ceremonial, the sentimental, the militant, the Elevated Discourse, the earthy and pungent, the exact and tightly argued. Of course, like all languages under twentieth-century conditions it is borrowing a great many new words. It is my impression that more words are borrowed from the international vocabulary of Greek and Latin derivation than from any one language like Russian or Chinese. Not infrequently a word is borrowed for a time and then dropped. Years ago Mongols in Outer Mongolia used to say "aeroplan," while those in Inner Mongolia used the Chinese word, *fei-chi;* now most people use a Mongol word meaning simply "the thing that flies."

Language, in a revolutionary period or any time of rapid change, can be an instrument of tremendous power, because it is in language that both the cold, fact-finding, reasoning intellect and the hot, unreasoning emotions express themselves. I will here give only one example. In the Mongol language only a few decades ago there was no word for "exploitation," because the society was not an investing or venture-enterprise society. Aristocrats and monasteries were well off because they had the right to collect tribute in kind, in labor, and in money from people who were born to pay tribute. If princes and Living Buddhas were easy-going, they were "good." If they were harsh, they were "oppressors"; but they did not manipulate investments, wages, and profits.

In the international vocabulary, which includes the Russian word *eksploatatsiya,* everybody except a few pedants has forgotten that the original late-Latin term meant simply "an unfolding." That is to say, you opened up the question in order to see what could be done about it. Because of this, "exploitation" in the international vocabulary is an ambivalent term. If you say, "Let us exploit this mine," it is "good." If you say, "let us exploit these miners," it is "bad." Apart from the mere hoarding of wealth, Mongolia had had only usury capital of a medieval kind. Even trade, especially retail trade, was a twin activity of usury, because of the practice of giving the consumer credit at usurious interest. As in all medieval societies, the usurer was hated. A man only went to the usurer because he was already in trouble, and if your debtor is already in trouble you keep a sharp eye on him and turn on the pressure mercilessly to make him keep up his payments.

It is not surprising, therefore, that, out of the vocabulary of herdsmen and hunters, which as Kowalewski says is the basic stock of Mongol speech, the Mongols came up with the expression *soron möljikh,* the exact meaning of which is "to drag toward oneself and gnaw like a bone." When in our language one man says to another that "Katanga is an area of capitalist exploitation," the expression has a wide variation of possible meaning, according to other things that may be in the minds of both speaker and listener; but when one Mongol says to another, "the capitalists are dragging Katanga toward themselves and gnawing it like a bone," the meaning is not in doubt. The speaker means, and the listener understands, that what is going on in Katanga is politically and economically bad and morally repulsive. And when such forms of speech are applied to a whole range of activities, the use of language has a double effect on the individual and the society. In a single discussion, the purpose may be the exchange of information; but every time the subject is mentioned there is a repetitive effect of indoctrination.

Changes in language are only part of what is happening in the world of the mind in Mongolia. My wife and I have been in Poland and Czechoslovakia as well as the Soviet Union, and of course we have heard Marxism discussed in many countries in Europe as well as in our own country, but Mongolia was our first experience of a battlefield which Marx has conquered without a battle.

Marx, Engels, and Lenin were all born into the middle class. They hammered out their beliefs and their principles of action only after they had decided what was wrong in that which was accepted as right in the families into which they were born. Marxism, or Marx-Leninism, came out of debate, and the debate is still going on. Even in Russia, which has been under a Communist government and Communist-directed system of education for so long, there is constant argument about "bourgeois survivals," and of course much more so in Poland and Czechoslovakia. The debate goes on because in the middle of the twentieth century capitalism and communism—or rather socialism, since there is no Communist society in operation anywhere—can do the same "modern" things: industrialize production, mechanize agriculture, interpose the power of the state to limit incomes, provide social services, proclaim high and altruistic principles, and reward the individual with prestige based on pride in having done well for the community, not just for oneself. The question under debate is which system can do all these things better, and with improvements could do them still better.

In Mongolia there is no such debate. I have referred before to the fact that there was no Mongol middle class, only an alien Chinese middle class (at a low stage of "bourgeois" efficiency), which was disliked and driven out, and which nobody would want to see back. To try to debate whether a ruling class of feudal princes and Living Buddhas could industrialize, mechanize, and modernize better than a Socialist government would be ridiculous. To debate whether a Mongol middle class could have been created, and if created could have done

better than the People's Revolutionary Party and the
present government, is to argue at a disadvantage, because the Mongols have had no contact with a progressive middle class or an efficient capitalism. The middle
class of Tsarist Russia was no great shakes, and in any
case the best representatives of the middle class and the
"bourgeois intelligentsia" in Siberia were the political
exiles, who were all anti-Tsarist, even those who were
not Bolsheviks. The Chinese ruling class and middle
class of war lords, landlords, and merchants was even less
attractive.

Nor does the Lama Buddhist religion offer an alternative revelation to the Mongol intellectual or the Mongol
who has a warm feeling for his fellow man. In the United
States we have a community of several hundred families
of Kalmuk Mongols, adherents of this religion. In their
old homeland in Russia, near Stalingrad (now Volgo-
grad), the religion was dying out fast. When these refugees settled in America as displaced persons, the religion
revived, because it became the symbol and vehicle of
community loyalty and mutual help during the difficult
period when individuals and families were adjusting to
a new language, new kinds of employment, and new
living conditions. It remains to be seen whether, in the
American environment, the religion can perpetuate
itself by recruiting a new generation of young lamas.

In Mongolia, the religion has no such appeal. In the
nineteenth century it did not go through the searching
debates about, and sometimes difficult adjustment to, the
new discoveries and theories of science that shook the
Christian churches but, once the adjustments had been
made, left them better fitted to survive in the twentieth
century. It is therefore burdened with cosmogonic and

cosmological dogmas which are of antiquarian interest
but not compatible with scientific thinking, and ramify
into obscurantist notions of physics, chemistry, medicine,
and so on. It shut itself off even more tightly from the
intellectuals by its insistence on the Tibetan language.
In this it was regressive even by its own standards. The
great translations into Mongol of the evangelizing period
were forgotten, and a shabby standard was tolerated
under which a few scholars really mastered the Tibetan
texts, but hordes of lamas, using the Tibetan alphabet
phonetically, were only able to gabble the prayers without understanding them.

When laymen attended a service in a temple or monastery, they came to be awed and to bask in some kind of
divine or magical emanation from the ritual, sometimes
enhanced by the presence of a Living Buddha. There
was no such thing as a sermon, delivered in the common
language, exhorting people to good conduct or charity.
The religion taught that for a man to make himself
poor, at the expense of his family as well as himself, by
giving all to the church was "good." It did not teach that
the church had any obligations toward the society in the
way of charity, of secular education, of care for the sick,
the aged, or the orphaned. Indeed, it could not teach
any such thing, for these activities were of this world,
and it was a basic doctrine that religion is not of this
world but stands against it, holding up the ideal of
Nirvana, the ultimate escape from the Material into
Extinction.

In all churches, however, principles have to be accom-
modated to the routine of organization, and since Lama-
istic Buddhism was willy-nilly in this world, though in
principle not of it, there seems to be no recorded instance

of renunciation of the revenues and power that flowed toward the church. Individual renunciation, yes, as in the life of the hermit, but not institutional renunciation —one has to be practical. The outcome was that the church became in part the rival, in part the prop, of the hereditary feudal system. They stood together and fell together.

One of the most important weaknesses of the old religion was that, unlike Christian religions which oppose Marxism, it was not closely associated with the family. It was in fact hostile to the family. The best way to teach a boy religion was to take him away from the family and put him in a monastery, not to teach him in the family. The church regarded sex as sinful. Marriage is a regularization of sex relations. Therefore, the church only tolerated marriage at a distance, and did not sanction it with a religious ceremony. Some lamas even believed that homosexuality is less sinful than sex relations between man and woman, because it does not lead to procreation and thus to the perpetuation of sin.

A number of things did not go along with the old religion which do go along with Marxism, and ought to be easily understood by us because they also went along with Christianity when Protestant Christianity was knocking at the doors of modern China, India, and other countries. A turn-of-the-century American diplomat, John W. Foster (grandfather of John Foster Dulles), remarked approvingly that "... the teaching of Christianity tended to the introduction of ideas hostile to the existing governmental order and struck at ancestor worship. The missionaries opposed such native customs as slavery, concubinage, support of heathen festivals, and foot-binding. In fact, in China, as elsewhere and in all ages, the influence of Christianity was revolutionary." *

Many a Chinese used to say, "I am a Christian. Therefore I do not bind my daughter's feet and I treat my
wife as an equal. Therefore I am a progressive, modern
man." In much the same way, many a Mongol equates
Marxism with progressiveness in general, with keeping
clean, with not believing that prayer will cure sickness.
It is taken for granted that the ethics of a Marxist society
are of a higher order than the old religious ethics.

Another tendency has become very strong since the
Second World War. As countries become politically independent, they also want to develop economically. If
you are going to modernize, why not start with the
most modern? In many countries this has become a
strong argument for variants of socialism, state capitalism, or at least economic controls and state planning,
with the rejection of untrammeled free-enterprise capitalism as not modern.

These historical tendencies have their equivalents in
revolutionary Mongolia; but they are more than tendencies—they are the main tide of thought. There is no
continuing debate against surviving doctrines and no
fear of new competitors. The few remaining lamas can
be tolerated and even subsidized by the state, because
their beliefs have become an abstraction, no longer
linked up with the material interests of a group or class
within the society. The importance of Buddhism in the
history of Mongolia is officially recognized, and young
scholars on government stipends master several languages in order to study it more deeply, but their study
is no more likely to build up a body of believers and

* John W. Foster, *American Diplomacy in the Orient,* Boston,
1903, p. 411.

followers than if they were studying the cult of Osiris.
In the same way the young economists who study classical economics think of it as an abstraction in their own
country and of practical importance mainly for the
understanding of foreign coutries. In Mongolia there
is no cohesive group to whom capitalism would appeal
as a way of improving its lot.

On the political side this absence both of challenge
from the past and competition with alternative theories
of organization makes Mongolia different from other
"people's democracies." We usually dismiss as immaterial
the fact that the Polish Workers' Party is so called because
it was formed by coalition with former socialists, while
in China the government recognizes the representatives
of several minor parties. This is nothing but camouflage,
we say; but I think we are wrong. Communists do not
make unnecessary compromises. If the Poles and Chinese
and others make these adjustments, it is because they
recognize that there arc survivals in their societies which
are strong enough to need to be taken into account.
There is a continuing debate. There is a surviving generation which was brought up to think in non-Marxist
and anti-Marxist ways, there are people who pay only
lip-service to Communist doctrines, and there are,
I strongly suspect, people who sincerely consider themselves Marxists but really are not able to think in a completely Marxist way because their minds were moulded
by a non-Marxist upbringing.

Mongols are therefore justified in thinking that they
hold a unique position in the Communist world and are
senior to the Poles, Chinese, and others in having a
government based on Marxist theory, and also different
from the Russians, because Russia had a capitalist past

and Mongolia did not. For forty years, the People's Revolutionary Party has been the only organized party, and for more than twenty years it has not had to deal with any serious ideological challenge. The official doctrine of the Party not only claims this degree of seniority, but goes on to assert the importance of Mongolia's example and experience for newly independent countries in Asia and Africa *—especially those in which also capitalism was a foreign intrusion, associated with the era of colonial imperialism, and not part of their own history.

As in Russia, Marxist uniformity and Party discipline lead to a lot of awfully dull writing in the narrow field of politics and economics. Party histories, programs for the future, the official ideological expositions and justifications of programs, newspaper "how to interpret the Line" articles, exegetical pronouncements on the transition from feudalism to socialism without passing through capitalism, and all that kind of thing are dry, labored, pedantic. There is real intellectual interest, however, apart from the style of exegesis, in such concepts as organizing and planning the passage from one evolutionary stage in the history of society to another without passing through an intermediate stage. With this goes the idea of planning a program in development economics for the purpose of really catching up, not just imitating, and this I also find absorbingly interesting. The claim that newly independent countries can learn a lot from Mongolia is not mere boastfulness.

In the wider reaches of intellectual life—history, sociology, literature, art, music—I have the impression that lack of competition from other systems of ideas leads to

* D. Tömör-Ochir, in *Forty Years.*

a good deal of rather naïve Marxism. I hope the many friends I made in Mongolia will not think that I intend this in any slighting or patronizing way, because the truth is that I find it rather refreshing. For example, Marxism emphasizes the mode of production and class conflict. The Mongol scholar says, "Why, of course. Our mode of production was pastoral, that of the Chinese was agricultural. No wonder we were different. And as for class conflict, let us look for it in the career of Chingis Khan and for differences in class structure before and after Chingis."

Up to this point, I think the approach is valid. What Marxists call a "mode of production" is often what Americans call a "way of life"; or at least I cannot think of a way of life that does not include a mode of production. I think it is naïve, however, to oversimplify and to go too far. To take only one example: I doubt very much whether the tribal wars of Chingis Khan's youth can be explained by saying that "bad" chiefs led "good" people, who would otherwise have been peaceful and harmless, to capture and plunder each other. I suspect that many a young warrior from the common people went off to war with great zest. But I must add that the leading scholars in Mongolia are not naïve at all. The way in which a Damdinsüren can analyze the "feudal" and "popular" elements in an old Mongol chronicle is a model of exact scholarship and fresh, individual thinking.

Without reading, seeing, and hearing a lot more I should hesitate to speak as an authority on novels, short stories, poetry, painting, the theater and opera and the cinema, but my impression is that the Mongols have suffered less from the banalities of "socialist realism" than the Russians. If I am right, then I suspect that the reason may be that the dull and boring qualities of "socialist realism" can be ascribed in part to a propaganda pressure to convince Russians that all kinds of things formerly done or believed in or accepted as right in a bourgeois way within a bourgeois society ought to be made over in a socialist way within a socialist society. But not only had the Mongols never had a bourgeois society; they had never had some of the things that exist in both a bourgeois society and a socialist society.

The Mongols had had religious sculpture but no decorative sculpture for homes or monumental sculpture for public places; they had had religious painting but no representational or abstract painting. They had had folk music, court music, and religious music, but no orchestral music, and no instrument as complicated as a piano or organ. They had neither opera nor ballet. They had had religious pageants but no theater. They had had wonderful epic poetry and folk poetry, but no lyric or romantic poetry. They had no novels or short stories (though one Mongol in Inner Mongolia had written a famous novel in the Chinese manner which exists in both a Chinese and a Mongol version).

"Socialist realism," therefore, though imitated, seems to me to have been subordinated to a Mongol renaissance, an extraordinary outburst of creativeness and intellectual vigor. For the Mongols the real problem often was not whether a thing should be done in the bourgeois way or the socialist way but whether it could be done by Mongols at all. The mastering of new techniques and genres—leaping instead of evolving into the twentieth-century intellectual world, had for the Mongols the excitement of creative effort, even when it was imitative. Translation was one of the intellectual fer-

ments, and it would be absurd to think that only propagandistic material was translated. In any case, that which
has a propagandistic tendentiousness related to a particular phase wears off, while the great intellectual stimuli
have not only initial impact but enduring influence.

Both Pushkin and Shakespeare have been translated
and staged. A photograph of one of Mongolia's leading
operatic stars in the role of Othello was prominently
hung in public places in the summer of 1961. And
D. Natsagdorj, one of the translators of Pushkin—himself
sometimes called "the Mongol Pushkin," both because
of the beauty of his poetry and his versatility—also translated Edgar Allan Poe's *The Gold Bug*. If you are an
American, you may well ask, why Poe? And if Poe, why
The Gold Bug? The answer is, I think, that the Mongols
were—and still are—exploring in all directions.

I do not think, however, that exploring in all directions has the significance, in Mongolia, that people try
to attach to some article or speech in Poland or Russia,
on the chance that it may reveal the seeds of a revolt
against "thought control" or "brain-washing." In Russia, Poland, and other countries there are survivals of
democratic-capitalist ideas, and sometimes these ideas
are associated with family or personal memories of
favored status and an easier life. In Mongolia there are
virtually no such associations. There never was more
than a handful of princely families, and the princely
past is now as remote as the Middle Ages.

Probably the Mongol scholar most widely known
abroad is Professor B. Rinchen, a man of Elizabethan
versatility. He publishes poetry in Czech, which is only
one of his many languages, and he is also a novelist,
dramatist, and author of film scenarios. Some of his most

important scholarly work is published in West Germany. In Mongolia, Professor Rinchen is also known for his independence and individualism, both in politics and in scholarship (he has publicly criticized the new official alphabet, adapted from the Kyrillic, as not meeting proper linguistic standards). He has had his brushes with the regime, but he was also a favorite of the late Choibalsang, who admired his nationalistic fervor in reviving old Mongol cultural themes, and he wrote the script and supervised the historical staging and costuming of a highly nationalistic film, presenting "good" nobles as well as "bad" nobles, which is still shown. When the old Committee of Sciences and Higher Education was raised in 1961 to the status of an Academy of Sciences, Dr. Rinchen was one of the first Academicians appointed. In the context, it would be absurd to suggest that, when Dr. Rinchen publishes some of his most important work in a country known for its hostility to the Soviet Union, it is in any way comparable to smuggling out the text of a *Dr. Zhivago* to be published abroad. For Mongols, it means that Mongol scholarship stands on a footing of international equality.

Several Europeans who were in Ulan Bator in 1961 wondered whether the present enthusiasm for Russian ballet, opera, and music might not contribute to a subordination of the Mongol culture to the Russian culture. The truth is that the cultural adaptation is rather complicated. In all these arts, the Russians themselves have been influenced by Oriental and especially Central Asian cultures; this is one of the reasons why Russia is different from the West in its ballet, opera, and music. The Mongols know this, and find it intellectually stimulating. For them, the mastering of these techniques goes beyond simple "adaptation to" Russian culture; it is rather their own readaptation of that which others had previously adapted.

In the same way, it has long been known that the special Chinese theatrical form called "Peking opera" was very strongly influenced by the Mongols during their period of rule in China in the thirteenth and fourteenth centuries. But just what were the influences, and to what extent were they blended, perhaps, with Persian and other non-Chinese influences? Mongol scholars today are attempting to show that a very difficult research problem can be handled by a Mongol student of Chinese history and culture as well as, or better than, by a Chinese student of Mongol history and culture. Mongols scorn the idea that their culture is so inferior that it always was and still must be a taker and never a giver.

At Tsetserleg, on our way west from Ulan Bator, my wife and I saw a film, the title of which can be freely translated as "Horseback is All Right." It opens with two young men, good-natured rivals. One revels in the old life and the old ways. He can ride the wildest horse, is clever with the Mongol pole-lasso, a skilled horseman. The other has a motorcycle and is the partisan of everything new.

Enter The Girl, very pretty. She is driving the new ambulance which the negdel has just acquired. At once the rivalry between the two young men reaches, to put it dialectically, a "higher plane." They go into a frenzy of competition, each one showing off his prowess in his own line. Anyone who has seen a few old Soviet films knows the answer. The machine triumphs. The inadequacies of the old, backward way of life are shown up. But wait.

The Girl is driving her ambulance across country—
not too fast, because there is no road, only cattle trails.
Horseback is All Right gallops besides her, showing off
and showing that a machine is not all that much better
than a horse. Now he is ahead, now alongside, now behind. His horse steps into a hole and falls, breaking its
neck. The Girl stops and offers him a lift home. Discon-
solate but proud (he loved that horse), he refuses the lift
and trudges home, saddle on shoulder.

The next day, without a horse, he has to go out herding yaks. He rides a yak. People jeer at him. But then
The Girl, out driving her ambulance again, stalls at the
ford of a small stream. Wheels spin. Car can't make it.
Mr. Motorcycle comes along. That's simple. He hitches
a tow-rope, to tow the car out—no good. Car and motorcycle together can't make it. It is the turn of Horseback
is All Right. He hitches up a couple of yaks and tri-
umphantly pulls the ambulance out.

There are more sequences of ups and downs, including some to prepare the audience for the New Morality
by showing that the affections of Motorcycle are not as
stable as those of Horseback is All Right. Motorcycle
will fall for any girl, if she's in some new kind of a job.
Horseback is All Right is a bit dumb, but he's a dependable type.

Then the grand climax. Blizzard—sensationally photo-
graphed. The cattle stampede, running before the storm.
If they aren't turned, they'll scatter, and the losses will
be disastrous. Engine roaring, Motorcycle dashes off,
depending on speed. Snowdrift. That's the end of that.
Horseback is All Right, slower but riding with courage
and skill, knows his cattle. Don't frighten them, but turn
them, turn them. He rounds them up. Situation saved.

My memory is a bit blurred here: I was having such a good time laughing. But I think that Motorcycle has to be rescued and that both Horseback is All Right and The Girl have a hand in it. Anyhow, Motorcycle is no longer *deus ex machina,* but *machina* is still in it, as the ambulance—but the one who gets The Girl is Horseback.

Moral: Don't get mixed up over this controversy about whether the old is better than the new, or the new better than the old. We need both. Marry them to each other.

A wonderful country, Mongolia, and the Mongols are wonderful people.

A note on sources and supplementary reading

IN WRITING THIS BOOK I have kept footnotes to a minimum, because most of my new material is from Mongol and Russian sources. Fortunately, however, Mongolia is by no means a closed country, and fairly recent material is also available in other languages. A number of the books listed below have bibliographies, which widen the field indefinitely for those who want to go on reading about Mongolia.

IN ENGLISH

National Economy of the Mongolian People's Republic for Forty Years, A Collection of Statistics, Ulan Bator, 1961. There are two editions, one in Russian and English, one in Mongol and Russian.

Harrison Salisbury, *To Moscow and Beyond,* New York, 1960. The author is a correspondent of the *New York Times.*

Gerard M. Friters, *Outer Mongolia and Its International Position,* Baltimore, 1949. (Introduction by Owen Lattimore.) The most useful summary of treaties, diplomatic notes, and official statements.

Ivor Montagu, *Land of Blue Sky, A Portrait of Modern Mongolia,* London, 1956.

Ma Ho-t'ien, *Chinese Agent in Mongolia,* translated by John DeFrancis, Baltimore, 1949. (Introduction by Owen Lattimore.) An important Chinese account of Mongolia in the years 1926-27, which were critical for both Mongolia and China. Although the author was there on a mission for the Left Wing General Feng Yü-hsiang, he was also connected with the Right Wing intelligence service of the Kuomintang.

Andrew J. Grajdanzev, *A Japanese View of Outer Mongolia,* translated and condensed from a Japanese book by Yasuo Misshima and Tomio Goto, New York, 1942. This mimeographed publication of the Institute of Pacific Relations is the only available account in English of what the Japanese knew and thought about Mongolia in the 1930's.

Owen Lattimore, *Nationalism and Revolution in Mongolia,* New York and Leiden, 1955. I list this principally because it contains the only translation into English, by Owen Lattimore and Urgungge Onon, of a book by a modern Mongol historian—the *Life of Sukebator* by Sh. Nachukdorji (the new Kyrillic spelling is Natsagdorj).

A magazine article, recent and outstanding in quality, is William O. Douglas, "Journey to Outer Mongolia," in the *National Geographic,* March 1962.

Newspaper files can also be consulted. In 1957 the *New York Times* had despatches from Mongolia by Jack Raymond, and in 1959, and again in 1962, from Harrison Salisbury. In 1961 the *Wall Street Journal* had despatches from Igor Oganesoff. In 1961 also Reuter's Agency of London and Agence France-Presse of Paris had correspondents in Mongolia, Mr. Clare McDermott and M. Jules Joelson.

In German and French

Erich Thiel, *Die Mongolei: Land, Volk und Wirtschaft,* Munich, 1958. This excellent handbook has a great deal of practical, detailed information on both the pastoral economy and the agricultural development of Mongolia, and is one more reminder

of the intense interest of West Germany in the economic potential
of Mongolia—and of the Soviet Union and China.

I. J. Slatkin [I. Ya. Zlatkin], *Die mongolische Volksrepublik*,
Berlin, 1954. I list the German translation because I do not have
the Russian original.

Herrmann Consten, *Weideplätze der Mongolen im Reiche
der Chalcha*, Berlin, 1919. A frequently sensationalized and sometimes garbled but still interesting account of Mongolia in the
period of the 1911-12 revolt against China. Some striking photographs of important political figures of the time.

Erich Haenisch, *Die geheime Geschichte der Mongolen*,
2nd ed., Leipzig, 1948. The pioneer and still the most serviceable
translation of the famous *Secret History of the Mongols*. There is
also a French translation which the late Paul Pelliot left uncom-
pleted at his death. An important English translation is now at
last expected, from Professor Francis W. Cleaves, of Harvard. It
will be accompanied by full historical and textual criticisms.

Pavel Poucha, *Die geheime Geschichte der Mongolen*,
Prague, 1956. Not a translation, but a valuable commentary, by
a Czech scholar. It assembles material from the *Secret History*
under various headings for historical, economic, and social analysis. Being a pioneer work of its kind, it is open to challenge here
and there, but it reveals how much treasure of the past is hoarded
in this absorbing chronicle.

René Grousset, *Le Conquérant du monde, vie de Gengis-
khan*, Paris, 1944. The best modern biography of the great con-
queror; but a new one is now very much needed.

IN CHINESE

B. Shirendyv and others, *Meng-ku Jen-min Ko-ming San-
shih Nien* (Thirty Years of the Mongolian People's Revolution),
2nd ed., Peking, 1953. I list this Chinese translation because I do
not have the Mongol original. Useful for specialists, for comparing the official thirty-year (1951) and forty-year (1961) evaluations
of the record in Mongolia.

IN RUSSIAN

B. Shirendyb, *Narodnaya Revoluyutsiya v Mongolii i Obra-zovanie Mongol'skoi Narodnoi Respubliki,* 1921-24, (The People's Revolution in Mongolia and the Formation of the Mongolian People's Republic, 1921-24), Moscow, 1956. There is no indication whether this was first published in Mongol. The author is now President of the Mongolian Academy of Sciences.

Istoriya Mongol'skoi Narodnoi Respubliki, (History of the Mongolian People's Republic). A collective work by a group of Mongol and Russian historians. The various chapters or essays, which deal with remote as well as recent history, are not individually signed.

Mongol'skaya Narodnaya Respublika, (The Mongolian People's Republic), Moscow, 1952. A collection of articles by Russian authors.

I. Ya. Zlatkin, *Ocherki Novoi i Noveishei Istorii Mongolii,* (Essays in the Modern and Recent History of Mongolia), Moscow, 1957. Particularly good for the eighteenth century, in which the Manchus extended their conquest from northern to western Mongolia.

I. M. Maiskii, *Mongoliya Nakanune Revolyutsii,* (Mongolia on the Eve of Revolution), Moscow, 1959. A revised edition of the author's famous and now almost unobtainable *Sovremennaya Mongoliya,* (Contemporary Mongolia), Irkutsk, 1921. Academician Maiskii, as the head of a mission from the Siberian Co-operatives, which was trying to develop trade before the Mongolian Revolution of 1921, had unique opportunities for observation. Later, Mr. Maiskii (Ivan Maisky) made a favorable impression in England in the 1930's as the very able Soviet Ambassador to the Court of St. James's.

Kh. Choibalsan, *Izbrannye Stat'i i Rechi,* (Selected Articles and Speeches), Moscow, 1961. A short selection, from a very much larger total (there are at least four volumes in Mongol), in Russian translation.

G. I. Mikhailov, *Ocherk Istorii Sovremennoi Mongol'skoi Literatury*, (A Sketch of the History of Contemporary Mongolian Literature), Moscow, 1955. Contains information about the work and careers of D. Natsagdorj, Ts. Damdinsüren, and B. Rinchen (all mentioned in this book), and, of course, much other material. Interesting comments on Mongol critics and criticism, which reveal, in one phase after another, how the "official line" in the Soviet Union was handed on to Mongolia.

D. Natsagdorj, *Izbrannoe*, (A Selection), Moscow, 1956. Examples, in translation, of the verse and prose of this appealing and romantic young genius, who was also unsurpassed in his realistic sketches. Two short introductions, one by V. A. Lugovskii and one by Ts. Damdinsüren.

IN MONGOL

Mongol ardyn khuv'sgalt nam ba ardyn khuv'sgalyn döchin jil, (Forty Years of the Mongolian People's Revolutionary Party and the People's Revolution), by a group of authors, Ulan Bator, 1961.

MAKhN ikh, baga khural, töv khoroony bügd Khurluudyn togtool shiidver, (Decisions and Resolutions of the Great and Little Khurals and Plenary Sessions of the Central Committee), Ulan Bator, 1956. This is vol. I, for the years 1921-39. I do not know if the second volume has yet been published.

Yu. Tsedenbal, *MAKh namyn töv khoroonoos namyn XIV ikh khurald tav'san tailan iltgel, mön khurlaas gargasan togtool,* (Report presented to the XIVth Great Khural of the Party by the Central Committee of the Mongolian People's Revolutionary Party, and Decisions Issued by the Khural), Ulan Bator, 1961.

Ts. Puntsagnorov, *Mongolyn avtonomit üeiin tüükh,* 1911-19, (History of the Autonomous Period of Mongolia, 1911-19), Ulan Bator, 1955.

Mongol ardyn juramt tsergiin durtagaluud, (Narratives of the Mongolian People's Volunteer Army [Partisans]), Ulan Bator, 1961.

V. I. Lenin, *Mongolyn tukhai,* (On Mongolia) , Ulan Bator, 1960. A collection of excerpts in which Lenin referred to Mongolia on various occasions. In an appendix are two brief but interesting accounts: "On a meeting with Lenin," by B. Tserendorj, and "Lenin on the subject of the Mongolian Revolution," by B. Shumyatskii, whom Lenin sent to Mongolia in 1919, and who returned in 1920 with a delegation of "several Mongol revolutionaries."

J. Sambuu, *Malchdad ökh zövlölgöö,* (Advice to Herdsmen) , Ulan Bator, 1956. The author is President of the Republic.

Ts. Damdinsüren, *Mongolyn uran zokhiolyn toim,* (A Review of Mongolian Literature), Ulan Bator, 1957. This is vol. I, thirteenth to sixteenth centuries. Vol. II has not yet been published, so far as I know.

Ts. Damdinsüren, *Soëlyn övig khamgaal'ya,* (Let Us Defend Our Cultural Heritage), Ulan Bator, 1959. A small but important collection of reprinted articles, the earliest dated 1955.

* * *

I should perhaps add just a word or two about spelling. I have tried to be consistent, but not pedantic. "Ulan Bator" is now an internationally established form, even though the modern Mongol spelling is "Ulaanbaatar." Vowels and double vowels are the great problem for people who are not used to a language like Mongol. For example, "del" is "a horse's mane" but "deel" is "a gown." In "deel," the double "e" is not pronounced as in the English word "deal," but is somewhere between the "e" in "dell" and the "a" in "dale," dragged out to double length: "de-ell."

I have used a simple transcription, not trying to distinguish between the "straightforward e" and the "reversed e" of the Kyrillic alphabet. As for the other vowels, perhaps the simplest thing is to warn the reader that o and oo and u and uu are not pronounced exactly like English vowels, and ö and öö and ü and üü are not pronounced exactly like the German umlauted vowels, and let it go at that. Just remember that in any language, including our own, a letter is only an approximate, conventional guide to pronunciation. Also, when we say that in English a letter is "pronounced differently" in two different words, what we ought to say is that the same letter is used to represent two different sounds. This happens in Mongol, too.

Russian has no "-ng" at the end of a word, as we have in a word like "sang." When the Mongols adopted the Kyrillic alphabet, they adopted this pattern too. The old spelling of the name Choibalsang is with "-ng" at the end, and that is the spelling I have used in this book, but the new spelling is Choibalsan. In any case, the "g" comes back in the possessive case: "Choibalsang's" is "Choibalsangiin."

In the use of family and personal names, the Mongols are in a stage of transition. Until recently, only the personal name was used, and many people did not even know their family or "clan" name. Before the Revolution Tsedenbal, the Premier of Mongolia, would have been called just Tsedenbal, and nobody would have known or cared what his family name was. Now people use family names, but only as initials. Therefore the name of the Premier, for formal purposes like signing a book or a report, is given as Yu. Tsedenbal. This stands for Yumzhagiin (Yumjagiin) Tsedenbal. The "-iin" at the end shows that this name is in the possessive case. Therefore Mr. Tsedenbal's name means "Tsedenbal of Yumzhag." The reason for this is that sometimes people use their inherited clan name and sometimes they start a new family by just taking their fathers' personal name. Thus, Yumzhagiin may mean either "of the clan of Yumzhag" or just "son of Yumzhag" (like Williamson) . In any case, if you ever meet Mr. Tsedenbal, it will be perfectly polite to address him as Mr. Tsedenbal, not Mr. Yumzhagiin.

Index

Advice to Herdsmen, 45, 46, 47
agriculture, 26, 29-30, 32, 35-6, 39,
    40-42, 158-9, 161, 164-5, 189,
    193-4
    butter, 187
    cheese, 187
    dairies, 164
    grain, 26, 38, 39, 193
    haymaking, 168, 192-3
    irrigation, 26, 40, 193
    milk, 39, 69, 187
    millet, 38
    rice, 26
    wheat, 26, 29, 38
airplanes, 2, 125, 203
Albania, xv, 197
Allied intervention, *see* Siberia
Altai Mountains, 24
American Revolution, 92
Americans, *see* United States
Amur River, 11, 24
Anfu clique, 59, 60, 62
animals, *see* herding
archery, *see* sports
architecture, 146, 174
Arctic Ocean, 24

ard (arat), 55, 111
aristocracy, *see* nobility
Army, 66, 80, 82, 83, 84, 85, 88, 90,
    124, 125, 134, 135, 136, 144, 149,
    155, 167
    see also Red Army
art, 102, 214, 215
Australia, 112
automation, 177
automobiles, 96, 112, 124, 125, 178,
    179, 182, 183, 192, 220, 221
Ayush, 66

ballet, 216, 218
banks, *see* National Bank of Mon-
    golia
"Banners," 73, 87, 100, 125
Bat-Ochir, L., 166
Beard, Charles A., 92
Bodo, 98
Bolsheviks, 71, 72, 84, 86, 98
books, *see* publishing
Bronze Age, 162
Buddhists, *see* Lama-Buddhist
    Church, Living Buddhas, Urga
    Living Buddha

Buryats (also Buryat Republic), 8, 9, 10, 11, 60, 61, 76, 87, 205
butter, *see* agriculture

camels, *see* herding
capitalism, 97, 114, 123, 138, 139, 159, 160, 161, 171, 197, 207, 208, 209, 212, 213
cashmere, 49, 187
cattle, *see* herding
cavalry, 41, 42, 73
Chahar, 131
cheese, *see* agriculture
Chiang Kai-shek, xiii, 15, 108, 120, 133, 167
China
    Communist, xi, xiv, xv, 3, 15, 23, 40, 94, 97, 108, 109, 118, 120, 121, 132, 158, 167, 171, 174, 175, 197, 198, 199, 200, 213
    Nationalist, xii, xiii, 3, 7, 11, 14, 50, 53, 55, 59, 60, 62, 63, 64, 80, 93, 94, 108, 109, 114, 116, 117, 118, 119, 120, 121, 126, 131, 133, 151, 152, 153, 154, 167, 172, 176, 224
    pre-1911, xii, xx, 3, 5, 8, 9, 11, 12, 31, 32, 38, 42, 50, 52, 135, 203, 209, 211, 212; *see also* Manchu Empire, trade
Chinese economic influence, 3, 55, 65, 67, 68, 78, 79, 95, 98, 101, 104, 112, 113, 114, 117, 160, 161, 162, 208
Chinese invaders, 63, 72, 73, 74, 80, 84, 86, 87, 88, 90, 137
Chinese labor battalions, 2, 171, 197
Chinese settlers, 3, 13, 14, 52, 54, 55, 56, 58, 62, 63, 66, 67, 68, 69, 78, 95, 138, 163, 208

Chinghis Khan, xi, xx, 9, 17, 28, 40, 41, 64, 77, 80, 99, 179, 203, 204, 215
Choibalsang, 78, 79, 80, 81, 82, 84-5, 86, 88, 90, 94, 105, 119, 121, 127, 128, 129, 143, 148-69, 218
    see also "cult of personality"
Christianity, 65, 102, 115, 138, 139, 205, 211, 212
Chuluut River, 179
church, *see* Lama-Buddhist Church
clergy, *see* Lama-Buddhist Church
climate, 25-7, 29, 32, 34, 41, 42, 46, 158, 174, 184, 189, 220
coal, 158, 163-4
Cold War, xiv
collectives, *see* co-operatives
collectivization, 123, 124, 126, 127
Comintern (Third International), 89, 108, 109, 126, 127, 128, 129
Communist-ruled countries, xiv, xv, xvii, xix, xxii, 2, 46, 196, 197
co-operatives, 68, 95, 97, 108, 111, 112, 114, 117, 118, 122, 123, 125, 136, 137, 138, 145, 146, 147, 169, 175, 178, 185, 186, 191, 192, 194, 195
    negdels, 178-90, 193, 219
Cossacks, 9, 60, 63, 69, 79, 81
cows, *see* herding
"cult of personality," 79, 106, 130, 148, 149, 150, 154, 165, 166
culture, 203, 205, 214, 215-19
currency, 113
Czechoslovakia, xv, 23, 160, 167, 174, 175, 207, 208

dairies, *see* agriculture
Dalai Lama, 4, 105, 106, 131, 132
Dalan Dzadagad, 29
Dambadorj, 119, 120, 154, 155
Damdinsüren, Ts., 66, 203, 215

Decline and Fall of the Roman Empire, 31
Demid, 155
development economics, xv, xvi, xix, xxi, xxii, 97, 157, 158, 159, 160, 164, 168, 170-201, 212, 214
   see also industrialization
Dzabkhan River, 25

East Germany, 23, 175
Eastern Mongolia, 77, 78, 79, 84, 104, 124, 204
economic development, *see* development economics
economy, xv, 136
education, 3, 71, 76, 82, 83, 85, 96, 100, 102, 111, 130, 137, 146, 164, 168, 169, 170, 176, 177, 182, 190, 202
England, *see* Great Britain
ethnic stock, xii

"False Lama" (Dambijantsan), 18
Far Eastern Republic, 88
farming, *see* agriculture
feudalism, 3, 54, 55, 56, 57, 59, 83, 100, 103, 104, 106, 111, 128, 140, 208, 215
   see also nobility
films, 182, 217, 218, 219-21
fishing, 25, 36, 49, 158
Five-Year Plan (1961-65), 164
foreign policy, xiv, xv, 14, 15, 61, 62, 72, 90, 94, 95, 109, 110, 120, 128, 129, 141, 150, 151, 152, 153, 154, 155, 157, 166, 196, 197, 199-201
forests, 27, 111, 158
Foster, John W., 211
frontier concept, 23, 38, 52
fuel, 44, 163, 190, 191

Gandang, 146
geography, 23-9, 40, 42, 46, 110, 152, 158, 164, 174, 178, 179, 182
Germany, 59, 114, 135, 155
Gibbon, Edward, 31
goats, *see* herding
gobi, 27, 28, 29
grain, *see* agriculture
grazing, *see* herding
Great Britain, 11, 12, 13, 51, 52, 62, 92, 112, 114, 138, 139, 160, 176, 177
Great Wall, 12, 37, 38, 42
Gold Bug, The, 217

haymaking, *see* agriculture
Henry VIII of England, 6, 138
herding, 32-3, 35-6, 39, 57, 139, 163, 186
   artificial insemination, 194-5
   camels, 42, 47, 165
   cows, 32, 42, 43, 46, 47, 187, 189
   cross-breeding, 45, 193-4
   goats, 44, 187
   horses, 43
   livestock, 32, 36, 42, 46-8, 111, 123, 161, 164-5, 184-7, 189, 194
   mares, 188-90, 195
   Orkhon sheep, 45
   oxen, 42, 43
   sheep, 39, 44, 46, 186
   yaks, 32, 42-3, 187
history, *see* scholarship
horses, *see* herding
horse-racing, *see* sports
hospitals, *see* medicine
housing, 170, 174, 176, 182, 183, 184, 196
   tents (*gers*), 44, 183, 184
Howard, Roy, 134

Hsü Shutseng ("Little" Hsü), 60, 61, 62, 63, 80, 87, 89

India, xx, 13, 132, 156, 171, 203
industrialization, xix, 2, 16, 94, 158, 159, 160, 163, 164, 165, 172, 173, 175, 176, 177, 188, 191, 192, 193, 195, 208
  see also development economics
Inner Mongolia, xi, xiii, xviii, xxii, 1, 3, 4, 5, 6, 7, 9, 10, 13, 15, 17, 18, 20, 25, 30, 37, 38, 53, 56, 58, 59, 61, 67n., 115, 131, 132, 133, 134, 135, 136, 153, 155, 167, 184, 206, 216
intellectuals, 76, 85, 102, 139, 202, 209, 210
Irkutsk, 85
Iron Age, 162
irrigation, see agriculture

Japan, 12, 13, 51, 53, 93, 176
Japanese imperialism, xxi, 8, 12, 13, 15, 51, 53, 59, 60, 62, 63, 72, 87, 90, 94, 108, 118, 121, 124, 130, 131, 132, 133, 134, 135, 136, 137, 141, 144, 149, 153, 154, 155, 167
Jehol, 130
Joffe, A. A., 94
Jurchid (Chin) Dynasty, 204

Kalmuk Mongols, 209
Kara Khan, L., 94
Karakoram, 40, 178
Kazakhs, 32, 188
Kerulen River, 24
Khalkhyn Gol (Nomynkhan), 134
khangai, 27, 28, 47
Khangai, 179, 181, 190
Khitan (Liao) Dynasty, 204
Khotant, 179

Khubilai Khan, 203
Khubsugul Lake (Kossogol), 25
Kirghiz, 32, 188
Kobdo, 26, 71
Kowalewski, 204, 207
Kuiten, 24
Kuomintang, see China, Nationalist

Lake Baikal, 8, 24
Lama-Buddhist Church, 4, 5, 6, 53, 54, 55, 58, 59, 62, 65, 77, 78, 81, 86, 87, 94, 96, 99-103, 105-7, 111, 114, 115, 116, 133, 137, 138, 144, 163, 190, 204, 206, 209-11, 212
  lamas, 5, 6, 54, 62, 94, 96, 102, 103, 114, 116, 117, 125, 130, 136-7, 145-7, 211
  monasteries, 4, 5, 55, 58, 65, 100-102, 123, 125, 137, 145-6
  suppression of, 122-3, 125, 127, 130, 136, 137, 140, 145-7
  see also Living Buddhas, Urga Living Buddha
Lamyn Khure, 29
language
  Chinese, xi, xii, 1, 2, 76, 111, 119, 175, 205, 206, 216, 225
  Czech, 217
  English, xii, xviii, 76, 223-4
  Finnish, xii
  French, 204, 205, 224-5
  German, 224-5
  Greek, 205
  Khitan, 204
  Korean, xii, 1
  Latin, 205
  Manchu, xii, 205
  Mongol, xi, xii, xxii, 1, 2, 6, 45, 54, 67, 70, 71, 76, 81, 82, 111, 115, 137, 188, 203-7, 210, 216, 217, 218, 227-9

Russian, 1, 71, 76, 82, 204, 205, 206, 226-7
Sanskrit, 204
Tibetan, 6, 111, 137, 175, 204, 205, 210
Turkish, xii, 45
Larson, Franz ("Duke of Mongolia"), 115, 116
Latin America, 112
Left Deviation, 122, 126, 127, 128, 129, 130, 136, 137, 145, 149, 185
Left Wing ("Rural Opposition"), 118, 119, 120, 122, 127, 128
Lenin, V. I., 97, 104, 111, 149, 208
Lippmann, Walter, 157
literacy, see education
literature, 45, 46, 54, 140n., 214, 215, 216, 217, 218
    see also poetry
"Little" Hsü, see Hsü Shutseng
livestock economy, 164, 178, 187
    see also herding
"Living Buddhas," 4, 78, 101, 102, 111, 131, 206, 210
    see also Lama-Buddhist Church, Urga Living Buddha

machine and tractor stations, 192, 193
"Mad Baron," see Ungern-Sternberg
magazines, see publishing
Maksarjab ("Warrior of the West"), 79, 81
Manchu Empire, xii, xiii, xxi, 3, 4, 9-11, 13, 32, 50, 52, 59, 61, 67, 69, 79, 80, 101, 204
    see also China
Manchuria (Manchukuo), 12, 13, 24, 25, 36, 51, 60, 63, 72, 124, 130, 131, 132, 133, 134, 135, 136, 153, 167

manpower, 160, 167, 185
mare's milk, 19, 150, 188, 190
Marxism, xviii, 5, 11, 49, 64, 67, 97, 138, 149, 159, 197, 207, 208, 211, 212, 213, 214, 215
medicine, 100, 102, 105, 130, 168, 169, 176, 177, 182, 183, 184, 188
middle class, 3, 54, 55, 67, 95, 111, 114, 160, 208, 209
milk, see agriculture
mining, 161, 162, 163, 165, 175
minorities, 149, 176
monasteries, see Lama-Buddhist Church
Mongolian Academy of Sciences, xii, xvii, xx, xxii, 146, 174, 178, 218
Mongolian Revolution of 1911, xii, xiii, xiv, 3, 11, 13, 14, 50-74, 77, 80, 83, 85, 225
Mongolian Revolution of 1921, xiv, 14, 49, 71, 72, 73, 74, 75-91, 92, 93, 97, 105, 148, 151
    40th anniversary of, 50, 75-7, 150
Mongolian State Archives, 58, 64
Mongolian State Theater and Opera, 182, 183
Moscow, xvii, 174
movies, see films
music, 214, 215, 216, 217, 218

Nalaika, 164, 173, 177, 188
National Bank of Mongolia, 117
nationalism, 11, 51, 52, 53, 54, 55, 61, 62, 64, 65, 66, 67, 69, 72, 74, 79, 80, 86, 87, 88, 93, 96, 111, 133, 149, 150, 175, 200, 218
Natsagdorj, Dashdorjiin, xvii, 16, 217
negdels, see co-operatives

"New Turn," 124n., 129, 130, 136, 137, 148, 185
New York Times, 148, 223, 224
newspapers, *see* publishing
nobility, 3, 40, 41, 56, 58, 59, 62, 65, 73, 81, 83, 85, 87, 94, 96, 99, 100, 103, 104, 111, 114, 116, 121, 122, 123, 125, 153, 163, 195, 206, 208
    see also feudalism
nomadism, 16, 31-49, 118, 162, 186
    see also pastoral nomadism

Orkhon River, 24, 25, 40
Orkhon Turks, 41, 42, 203
Othello, 217

Panchen Lama (Banchin Bogd), 131, 132, 133
"Parliament," 62
Partisans, 18, 19, 72, 73, 75-7, 79, 80, 81, 86, 87, 96
pastoral nomadism, xx, 8, 31-49, 57, 58, 97, 161, 164, 165, 186, 187, 195, 215, 224
    see also herding, nomadism
"Peking opera," 219
Plebiscite of 1946, xiii, 15
Poe, Edgar Allan, 217
poetry, 17, 20, 205, 215, 216, 217
Poland, 23, 197, 204, 207, 208, 213, 217
police state, *see* security police
population, 23, 135, 152, 158, 164, 165, 173, 174, 183, 185, 186, 191, 195, 200, 202
post-stations, 57, 77, 82, 103
Pozdneev, 81
priests, *see* Lama-Buddhist Church
proletariat, *see* working class
publishing, xvi, 75, 81, 90, 126, 137, 164
purges, 98, 120, 121, 122, 123, 124,

125, 126, 127, 136, 138, 139-45, 155, 166
    rehabilitation of victims of, 99, 141, 148, 167
Pushkin, Alexandre, 217

railroads, 1, 2, 78, 164, 192
rainfall, 25, 26, 27, 28, 29, 33, 37, 40, 46, 165, 178
rebellions, 55, 56, 57, 58, 59, 66, 124
Red Army, 71, 73, 74, 87, 88, 89, 95, 125, 134, 135, 141, 151, 167
revolution, *see* Mongolian Revolution, Russian Revolution
Revolutionary Party (Mongolian People's R.P.), 75, 81, 82, 88, 97, 98, 103, 108, 109, 110, 118, 119, 120, 121, 122, 123, 124n., 125, 126, 129, 143, 145, 148, 149, 150, 151, 166, 181, 196, 209, 214
Revolutionary Youth League, 119, 120
rice, *see* agriculture
Right Deviation, 108, 118, 120, 121, 123, 128, 135, 139, 149
Rinchen, B., 217-18
"Rural Opposition," *see* Left Wing
Russia, *see* Red Army, Siberia, Soviet Russia, Tsarist Russia, White Russians
Russian Revolution, 52, 59, 60, 70, 73, 85, 86, 87, 88, 89, 113, 151, 154
Russo-Japanese War, 12, 51

Sain Shand, 29
Sambuu, J., 46, 47
"satellites," xiv, 135, 155, 156, 157
scholarship, xii, xix, xx, 5, 54, 66, 75, 89, 90, 102, 106, 111, 122,

128, 129, 140, 146, 204, 214, 215, 217, 218, 219
schools, *see* education
sculpture, 216
Secret History of the Mongols, 16, 17, 22
security police, 140, 141, 142, 144, 166
Selenga River, 24
Semenov, Ataman, 60, 63
Shakespeare, William, 217
sheep, *see* herding
Siberia, xxi, 1, 7, 8, 9, 10, 13, 23, 24, 27, 29, 35, 38, 58, 60, 62, 69, 70, 71, 72, 74, 76, 78, 80, 82, 85, 86, 94, 134, 167, 209
    Allied intervention in, 74, 87, 88, 89
Sinkiang (Chinese Turkestan), 26, 67, 80
"socialist realism," 215, 216
Sodnomdarjaa, 18, 19
Sorokovikov, 89
Soviet Russia, xi, xvii, 2, 8, 11, 23, 72, 74, 88, 93, 113, 119, 126, 130, 135, 141, 144, 148, 149, 151, 152, 154, 155, 156, 157, 164, 165, 168, 192, 197, 199, 200, 208, 209, 213, 214, 215, 216, 217, 218
    see also Red Army, Russian Revolution, trade
Soviet economic aid, xv, 29, 170, 171, 175, 176, 188, 193
Soviet foreign policy, xv, 14, 15, 93, 94, 96, 105, 108, 109, 110, 121, 134, 152, 153, 155, 198
Soviet influence, xi, xiv, xv, 14, 15, 52, 64, 65, 74, 82, 84, 85, 86, 88, 89, 90, 91, 94, 95, 97, 109, 110, 117, 118, 120, 121, 125, 126, 127, 128, 129, 130, 136, 139, 149, 154, 157, 166, 170, 171, 184, 191, 196, 218, 219

speculation, 112
sports, 16-23, 105, 219
    archery, 16, 22-3, 37, 38, 41, 150
    horse-racing, 16-20, 156
    wrestling, 16, 20-22
Stalin, Josef, 104, 128, 134, 141, 148, 149, 154, 155, 165, 166, 174
Suiyuan, 131
Sukebator (man), xvii, 1, 75, 78, 79, 80, 81, 82-4, 86, 88, 90, 97, 98, 104, 105, 119, 148
    (city), 2
Suman Gol, 179
Sun Yat-sen, 94, 104

Tariyat, 178, 179
taxation, 65, 123, 137, 164
Te Wang (Demchukdonggrob), 131
textiles, 45, 164
theater, 182, 215, 216, 217
Tibet, 4, 12, 13, 51, 52, 67, 116, 131, 139
    see also Lama-Buddhist Church
trade, 3, 30, 39, 40, 49, 114, 116, 117, 206, 207
    with China, 54, 78, 95, 96, 112, 114, 115, 117, 161
    with Russia, 54, 71, 78, 94, 112, 113, 114, 117, 136, 165, 168, 187
    with West, 112, 114, 116, 117, 161
translations, 204, 216, 217
Tsagaan Nur (White Lake), 179
Tsarist Russia, xii, 5, 8, 9, 11, 12, 13, 14, 32, 51, 53, 54, 59, 60, 69, 70, 71, 73, 76, 85, 161, 176, 209
    see also White Russians
Tsarist foreign policy, 10, 12, 13, 14, 51, 52, 53, 54, 59, 60, 71

Tsedenbel, Premier, 180
Tsetserleg, 178, 179, 219
Tukhachevskii, Marshal, 155
Tula River, 174

Ubsu Nur, 25
Ugedei, 40
Uighur Turks, 203, 204
Ulan Bator (Urga), 2, 7, 26, 29, 61, 62, 63, 68, 71, 74, 76, 78, 79, 80, 85, 119, 146, 156, 161, 163, 164, 173-5, 176, 182, 183, 188, 191, 195, 218, 219, 228
Uliassutai, 71
unemployment, 170
Ungern-Sternberg, Baron ("Mad Baron"), 63, 64, 74, 80, 87, 88, 89
United Nations, admission to, xi, xiii, 89
United Press, 134
United States, xiii, xiv, xvi, 15, 29, 59, 62, 92, 112, 114, 115, 156, 161, 167, 171, 189, 196, 197, 200, 209, 211, 217
Urga Living Buddha (Jebtsundamba Hutukhtu), 19, 53, 60,

61, 62, 65, 76, 77, 78, 80, 93, 98, 101, 104, 105, 106, 107, 108, 111, 115, 116, 125, 132, 133, 163
    see   also   Lama-Buddhist Church, Living Buddhas
Uryankhai (People's Republic of Tannu-Tuva), 76
Ussuri River, 11

Wall Street, 114, 115, 116
Wall Street Journal, 224
Wallace, Henry A., 7
Warsaw, 174
Western Mongolia, 18, 41, 55, 62, 77, 78, 79, 104, 124, 190
Wheat, see agriculture
White Russians, 60, 63, 72, 73, 87, 113, 151, 155
working class, 139, 161
World War I, 12, 59, 113
World War II, 7, 8, 14, 134, 135, 136, 166, 167, 212
wrestling, see sports

yaks, see herding
Yalta Conference, 15